American Education Abroad

Abroad

EDITED BY WILLIAM G. THOMAS

Macmillan Information
A Division of Macmillan Publishing Co., Inc.
NEW YORK

Collier Macmillan Publishers
London

Library of Congress Catalog Card Number 73-18517

International Standard Book Number 0-02-469910-1

Macmillan Information

866 Third Avenue
New York, N.Y. 10022

To my dad . . .

W.G.T.

CONTENTS

PART I

TRENDS, MOVEMENTS AND SYSTEMS OF OVERSEAS AMERICAN EDUCATION AND EDUCATORS 1

PART II

ROLES OF OVERSEAS AMERICAN EDUCATORS 79

PART III

FOREWORD

Education, U.S.-Style, has extended far beyond the country's continental boundaries. In its many overseas forms, it is as multi-faceted as it is from State to State. It differs in sizes and shapes, in content, and in constituencies.

Its purposes, however, are consistent. American education has moved abroad to provide a means of cultural inculcation and advancement and to assist young people to fulfill their respective potentials within both their own and other cultures.

INTRODUCTION

Education, throughout the world, is diverse.

It is diverse in organization, in administration, in financing, in staffing, in curriculum design, and in student population, among other unique distinctions.

Conversally, education, throughout the world, has much in common.

All nations are attempting to provide both for the aptitudes of their youth and the needs of their societies. All of them aspire to educate children, at the very least, to a level of education which will enable them to practice intelligent citizenship.

To consider both diversities and commonalities within the transplantation of one educational system, in its own infinitesimal varieties, into the systems of other countries is to consider the plight of American education overseas in its naked presence.

The authors of the eighteen chapters of this book have attempted to dissect this multi-fragmented plight according to their own terms and experiences, so that its various elements and compounds can be identified, comprehended, and tested by those who may have reason to follow, or perhaps, challenge, their advice and observations.

It is primarily due to the differences in educational systems that we have established hundreds of elementary and secondary schools and "campus abroad" branches of American colleges and universities. It is also due to these differences that we tend to look at one another's learning technologies to better our own. It is also due to these differences that international education is a reality.

To best view our own educational system beyond its confines, we must place it in its international education context.

Almost every form of instruction which ever existed, from the primitive imitative methods of prehistoric man (the Aborigines of Australia, the Indians of North American, among other examples), to the sophistication of instant-feedback, televised teaching machines and computer-assisted instructional devices, continues somewhere in the world today.

There are highly nationalized educational systems with centralized power vested in the government, where the control and coordination of all schools emanates. Such countries include France, Spain, Czechoslavakia, Albania, Bulgaria, Turkey, Italy, Austria, Poland, and the republics of the U.S.S.R.

There are also the partially or fully decentralized systems of education which have local or regional boards of citizens in control of education. West Germany, the United Kingdom, and the United States are among them.

Additionally, there are systems which mix educational responsibilities among national bodies, including Japan, the Scandanavian countries, and many South American nations. In such systems, the control of primary schools may differ markedly from that of secondary schools. Primary schools are the responsibilities of local communities, while secondary schools are governed by larger units of the populace.

Among other differences are the length of schooling and the kinds of primary and secondary schools available. The phases and methods of articulation between primary and secondary schools vary from country to country. There are different ways of financing education. There are different means by which individuals are trained to enter trades and technology. The education of teachers is also distinctive from country to country. There is variance in the interpretation of the purposes to which education should be addressed.

What are some of the practices and trends which are common to many countries? There is universal concern about the articulation between primary and secondary education, and between secondary and higher education. There is a desire to keep youth in school longer to learn more and delay their entry into the labor force. There is mutual interest in reforming secondary education and changing the administrative structures of educational systems. And, in many countries there has been a significant increase in the involvement of teachers in the training, review of qualifications, establishment of employment conditions, and the administration of educational organizations.

What are some of the differences? They are too numerous to describe with either fairness or accuracy. They are as varied as faces in a crowd.

However, in recognition of both educational differences and similarities, let us briefly consider the three levels of education individually within an international perspective.

Primary Education

In advanced societies, where education up to the age of fifteen may be compulsory, primary education can last up to eight years. This can occur in a primary school for five or six years and in a junior secondary school for two to three years. The junior secondary level may emphasize, either or both, academic or vocational education.

Several countries retain a rather traditional parallel division between primary and secondary schools where at age 10 or so, some are selected for a six to seven year academic preparation program to enter the university; some are selected for trade or vocational schools; while the rest continue in primary schools until the end of their compulsory education obligation.

In developing countries, one of the great problems is making even a minimum level of education available to young people. Many countries, particularly in rural areas, can provide only a two-year primary school. Others barely manage extremely modest four-year schools, situated far away from one another. In Latin America, for example, the scarcity of adequately trained teachers has often restricted schooling to the first two or three grades of primary education, even in centrally situated towns. Other schools may be one or two-teacher "all-grade" schools similar to those which were common in Europe and North American during the latter half of the 19th Century.

Secondary Education

In some countries, a problem of requirement examinations arises at the end of the point of entry to the junior secondary school, usually at age 11 or 12. The examinations either permit the selection only of the highest scoring students for whom places are available or they determine which students will go on to academic-preparatory schools and which ones will enter vocationally-oriented institutions.

In the United States and Canada, the organization of secondary schools is usually three years of junior secondary and three years of senior secondary school, after a six-year primary education. In Eastern Europe and Scandanavia, nine or ten-year compulsory schools consisting of primary and junior secondary levels, are followed by several different types of specialized senior secondary schools.

In several Western European countries, primary schooling lasts for four to six years; followed by partly specialized secondary schools whose courses may be six or seven years long and lead to the university or higher professional schools; or shorter, perhaps three to four years long, leading to work or to highly specialized vocational schools. In some cases, the degree of specialization is academic or technical. In other instances, there may be up to fifteen special schools: academic, technical, commercial, artistic, nursing, agricultural, teacher training, etc.

The comprehensive secondary school provides rather universal schooling or a basic general education to all children through their compulsory schooling. This is the case in the U.S.S.R. and other Eastern European countries and in the U.S., and many parts of Asia and Africa. The major organizational problem of the comprehensive secondary school is the provision of some type of specialized and vocational education. Currently, although an emphasis on academic preparation continues, vocational and "career education" courses are offered in parallel in the comprehensive secondary school.

In the developing countries, where both university preparation and vocational education are so important, serious difficulties are faced in providing adequate training for the skilled trades, scientific agriculture, and for many professional and administrative services.

At the completion of the senior secondary stage, all countries have some sort of selective machinery for determining which students are qualified to move upward to various types of higher education: junior colleges, universities, colleges, institutes of technology, and professional schools. There is a wide variety of methods in administering examinations or evaluating accumulated records, which may also serve as secondary school leaving requirements.

Some students are accredited by their own secondary schools to enter universities, while others must undergo nation-wide written scholastic examinations. In some countries, such as the Netherlands, though the Ministry of Education holds the responsibility for examinations, each school conducts its own. In New Zealand, the principal of a secondary school reviews a student's past academic history to recommend his entry to the university; other students, not so accredited, may take an external examination.

There are countries, such as the United Arab Republic, which hold national examinations and only those who score highest are admitted to the universities with the Ministry of Education allocating students to particular institutions and departments. In many countries, boards representing both schools and the universities conduct the examinations, as in the United Kingdom, with the universities making final selection of admittees. There are other varieties on these themes.

Private Schools

Organized private schools are not usually permitted in communist countries and some nations of Africa. In such countries, it is believed that private schooling is not based on the scientific concepts of the universal education programs which are in the best interests of cultural advancement.

The reverse is true in the Netherlands and Quebec, Canada, where the government supports both public and private schools, encouraging religious and community-oriented education.

Private schools exist in most countries, though their place in the educational spectrum varies in status. In some cases, they are considered as supplementary alternatives to public education, both saving money for the State and providing variety for those who so chose.

Higher Education

The third-level of education, higher education includes all institutions which require enrollees to have completed their secondary schooling. Higher education embraces two- and four-year colleges and universities, schools of higher technology, and those concentrating on high-level professional training in various fields.

In some countries, France, England, Germany, and Japan, among others, entrance to higher education is highly restricted. In others, such as the United

States, junior colleges and many state universities permit the entry of all students who are interested in further study beyond the secondary school, rather than those with the best academic backgrounds. In Sweden, two levels of higher education exist, one which is post-secondary and below university quality, and the other specific and restrictive.

United States Education Overseas

Due to the realities of the foregoing, it is obvious that wherever Americans go, American education is certain to follow.

Accordingly, the international, American community and dependent schools can have legitimate status in foreign countries, and except for dependent schools, can encourage the enrollment of children of host countries.

In higher education, such factors as language, enrollment restrictions of non-citizens, appropriate preparation, limited student space, nature of academic program, type of leaving degree, among many others, have made it more difficult for Americans to matriculate than for foreign students to attend colleges and universities in the United States. We have developed our own, very disjointed and random, unaffiliated networks of overseas branches of our higher educational institutions. There are a few small, private colleges and universities which cater to Americans, but they are largely non-accredited and limited in curricular offerings.

The United States has greatly influenced education throughout the world, just as its origins were the seedlings and roots of educational philosophies and practices of other nations. Our children, our teachers and administrators, and our researchers have taken our education, in its many forms, overseas. The winds of our educational trends, technologies, and tendencies have been blowing in every one of the earth's nations. American education has been – is – and will continue to exist overseas in its many guises. It is this existence to which we address ourselves.

PART I

TRENDS, MOVEMENTS, AND SYSTEMS OF OVERSEAS AMERICAN EDUCATION AND EDUCATORS

In colonial days, schools in this country were replicas of schools in Europe, particularly England. Although it was mandated in some Eastern colonies which established public town schools that all children be taught to read, most children only attended school for a very few years or not at all. In the Middle and Southern colonies, private and religious groups more often established schools. Our first colleges, Harvard, William and Mary, Yale, Princeton, among others, were modeled after England's Cambridge and Oxford. They were to produce "gentlemen scholars!" Beginning before the Revolutionary War, and gaining greater emphasis afterwards, new kinds of schools were created which gave a practical education aimed at preparing children for jobs in such fields as business, trade and navigation.

Realizing that separate private and religious schools could not provide the equality, unity, and freedom necessary for a new democratic nation, the States organized systems of public schools which would be equally open and free to everyone. A ladder system spread throughout the country which included elementary schools teaching fundamentals, high schools offering a comprehensive program for vocational development or further academic education, and State universities which emphasized the development of thinkers and leaders in a wide variety of disciplines.

Thus, once the follower in evolving educational programs, the United States became a leader in the creation of educational technology and methodology. Rather than advocating an elite system of education from which only a favored few would emerge, the country focused on mass education, financed by taxing its citizenry, seeking to develop basically educated individuals who would be directly able to contribute to the progress of the nation. For the most part, we have continued to pursue these idealistic concepts.

Each nation of the world has an educational system which is particularly unique to its needs, heritage, geography, economy, and its capabilities to deliver appropriate educational packages to its peoples. Most such systems, particularly in the newer and developing countries, were patterned after those of the countries which had colonized them, though greatly influenced by the missionaries and educational reformists. The educational leaders of these countries have long cast their eyes outside of their own systems to identify what is both good and transferable from the systems of other nations.

Many attempts at educational transplantation work, many do not. Following the Second World War, the attempt to structure the German and Japanese school systems after those of the United States proved almost futile.

1

There were too many cultural differences, historical and prior preferences which kept getting in the way; nor were enough teachers trained in the foreign educational methods to successfully make the transition and adaptation.

Accordingly, the influencing, borrowing, and dialogue, – the communicating between educators and leaders of various nations – has been done in the rarified atmosphere of friendly interchange.

We have exchanged students, teachers, and educational materials, and most importantly, ideas with many nations.

To have a communication base for cross-cultural educational exchange is healthy and essential. Thousands of American educators have worked overseas under the auspices of UNESCO, the Agency for International Development, religious organizations, the Fulbright Teacher Exchange Program, the Peace Corps, the United States Information Agency, to name only a few. In such capacities, they have primarily served at the invitation and within the existing educational systems of host foreign countries.

Scores of other Americans have worked abroad in American Dependent Schools and American Community Schools, which maintain typical curricula found in schools in the United States. Fewer Americans work in international schools which tend to amalgamate the best learning approaches from the many nations their students represent. Additionally each year American college and university students attend overseas branches of their home institutions or programs of foreign universities.

Thus the trends and movements of American education are relatively well known abroad, just as those of other nations are known in the United States. How do they become known? What are some of the newer trends? What are some of the influences? Have we or should we have major impact on international education? These are important questions.

What of our obligations to our own young citizens who, possibly due to the overseas employment of a father, must attempt to advance educationally with his peers at home? What are our systems of overseas education?

In response to these questions, I sought the aid of American educators who could best provide the answers, those who had been directly involved in overseas programs, those with the vision and expertise to look beyond their daily educational activities, to their implications, to impressions about them. I also welcomed their different styles of expression and have attempted to retain their freshness and uniqueness.

In an article which could be subtitled, "Where will my kids go to school during my overseas assignment?" Donald K. Phillips sets the stage with a dramatic vignette exemplifying similar discussions which occur in the United States everytime one faces the realities of overseas employment. He accurately describes the types, issues, problems, and nature of international schools only as one with his wide experience and intimate involvement with such schools can. In a practical, straight-shooting manner, he considers the quality of education, cultural shock, and financial conditions which affect and are affected by international schools. This loose "system" of overseas schools educates the largest number of American youth abroad next to the Dependent Schools coordinated by the Department of Defense.

The schools for the offspring of overseas servicemen and government employees are discussed in the chapter entitled "Will There Still Be Dependent Schools?" Geographically, the largest school system in the world, dependent schools are islands of United States culture within the boundaries of foreign nations. Their evolution, present status, and future are all addressed. A number of assumptions are made as to how both national and international circumstances will directly influence their directions and possible modifications which will have to be made in their organization.

Another large segment of American youth overseas participates in U.S. campus abroad programs. The great interest in educating college and university students outside the United States is evident in study programs, tours, and institutes offered through colleges and universities. Primarily concentrated in Europe, there are a number of overseas colleges and university branches and activities which are appearing in Asia, Africa, and South America. Such programs range from the seaboard campus of Chapman College to the several campuses abroad of the United States International University. They include the University of California with its more than twelve overseas study centers, as well as Middlebury College, which emphasizes learning languages in countries where the languages are spoken. Many overseas higher educational ventures have been in existence for years, while others have been developed recently to emphasize independent field work, urban, educational and governmental planning and study.

Most of the overseas academic programs are for juniors and seniors. They generally offer the same amount of academic credit a student would earn on his home campus. Sponsoring institutions handle all administrative processes and, usually, faculty members from those institutions provide most of the instruction abroad. William F. Sturner addresses what he feels to be essential features of an effective and successful educational experience in a foreign setting.

The interest, emphasis and involvement in international education on the part of the United States Office of Education is appraised by Robert Leetsma. He describes the history, legislative authority, and many programs sponsored by USOE. He addresses factors of difference, and project planning and participation. He specifically discusses exchange teaching, independent research, advanced language training, ethnic heritage seminars, and training and curriculum development projects. Certainly, one of the concerns of USOE is to reduce ethnocentrism in our own educational systems. Robert Leetsma defines ethnocentrism as a " . . . preoccupation with one's cultural subgroup, a lack of awareness of other cultures, of man in other settings, of different ways of being human." (from the official Office of Education appropriations hearings on OE's Fiscal Year 1973 budget request for excess foreign currencies, March 3, 1972.) This attitude is strongly reinforced in Leetsma's accentuating the interdependence of the nations in today's world.

Just as he might have written a personal letter to a friend, Robert J. Leach, long a leading figure in international education, begins his article with an overview of the overseas school programs of several nations. He, like Robert Leetsma, condemns ethnocentrism and concentrates on providing a rationale for a truly international school concept. He describes the potential benefits of an International Baccalaureate which would enable holders to enter higher education in any country of the world. He proclaims that calling schools "international" which are primarily reflections of particular national systems is wrong. His delightful article is present in this book because he points out in his own inimitable style both good and bad influences which U.S. education has had on the international scene.

This group of seven articles provides a backdrop of American education outside the United States brightly colored by its variety, scope, and its multipurposes.

Chapter 1

NEXT STOP: BUCARAMANGA – OR KUALA LUMPUR?

Donald K. Phillips

"Hello Bill – sit down. Cigarette?"

"No thanks, John – just finished one. Er, – you wanted to see me. What's up?"

"You!" The Senior Vice President beamed at him. "You're on the way up. And it's my pleasure to tell you about it."

Bill Stewart managed to keep his face reasonable immobile, but he grinned inwardly. At last, the breakthrough. The promotion he'd worked so hard for was coming. He thought of the happy smile on his wife Jill's face and the whoops of triumph from his three teenage kids when he brought the news home.

"Bill, we've been watching your work for quite awhile. In the half-dozen or so unforeseeable emergencies in your department these last two years, you demonstrated know-how, brains, self-control, a good sense of public relations, – and you won every time. We're convinced you're ready for managerial responsibility."

Bill looked at him. His thoughts spun. The only recently opened top spot was the one in marketing – but that job carried a vice-presidency with it!

"Bill, we're moving Henry Johnson into the vice-presidency in charge of marketing. He's been marketing and sales chief for the Near East-South Asia division for four years and has done a heluva good job. We want you to take his place."

Bill gulped, but still managed to keep his face straight, and said, "Headquarters in Beirut?"

"That's it" replied the VP, "a big jump in responsibility – a big jump in pay and benefits – and –" the man behind the desk grinned, "a training ground for the gold key to the Executive washroom on this floor! How's that for good news on a rainy Friday afternoon in January?"

Bill, still disbelieving, offered a humble, "Incredible."

"How soon do you think you and Jill could be ready to move? We'd really like to get Henry here within a month, and you'd have to be there well before he leaves for briefing and orientation." He clapped an arm around Bill's shoulder. "Break the good news tonight to Jill – talk over the nitty-gritty over the weekend – come in Monday morning ready for a planning session. Bill! It couldn't have happened to a nicer guy. Monday at ten – OK?"

Three weeks later – it was early February – Bill and Jill Stewart, with two sons aged seventeen and thirteen and a daughter of fifteen, plus a small mountain of luggage, landed in Beirut, Lebanon, to begin a new chapter in

5

their lives. The company had taken care of everything – house disposal back home – lovely home rented in Beirut – everything packed for shipment or storage – Lebanese house servants engaged to take care of them – car at their disposal – company guide to take charge of them at the airport – yes, everything efficiently arranged. Even the paper work for the children's transfer and admission to the American Community School in Beirut had already been processed. Yes, it was too bad that the kids had to be uprooted in the middle of the school year, especially with Bill Jr. just having made the basketball team, and with Mary Ellen just beginning to feel comfortable in high school. But weren't they lucky there was such a fine American School in Beirut?

$$* \quad * \quad * \quad * \quad * \quad *$$

The story of the Stewarts is repeated perhaps a thousand times a year in American business and government circles. They and the other families who face this sort of forced and sudden relocation are lucky that, in most of the faraway foreign places to which they may be assigned by business or the government, there is an American school for their children.

Relatively few Americans whose children go to school in Croton Falls, N.Y., or Bangor, Maine, or Bellevue, Ohio, have any idea that the presence of Americans on business or government assignment in every quarter of the globe has required the development of hundreds of "international" or "overseas" schools scattered all over Latin and South America, Africa, the Near and Middle East, Asia, and Europe. Just exactly how many of these schools there are is uncertain, for a few of them come and then go. Almost all of these overseas schools, however, are relatively stable. Excluding the several hundred U.S. Department of Defense schools operated for the children of service men assigned abroad, the list compiled by International Schools Services of Princeton, New Jersey, has just over three hundred. These schools are estimated to enroll about 150,000 children, to employ about 12,000 teachers and administrators, and to have combined budgets of approximately $125,000,000. Lumped in this fashion, it is a large operation, although its component parts may be small.

The average man in the streets of Wilkes Barre, Pennsylvania, or of Traverse City, Michigan, probably knows little about the world outside the United States, in spite of the World History course taken in high school. For children, such traditional studies as Geography as it was taught a half century ago has become blissfully watered down in "Integrated Social Studies" or "Survey of the World." Consequently, except for the relatively few who work in the international divisions of the few companies that do business aborad, such names as Dar-es-Salaam, Kinasha, Cochabomba, Bucaramanga, Zagreb,

Reykavik, or Kuala Lumpur just produce a dropping of the jaw and a stuttered, "...w-w-where in God's name is — w-what did you say — Cochabamba?!?" Yet hundreds of Americans live in these overseas cities. Located in each of them is an American U.S. sponsored school, enrolling 698, 640, 174, 220, 15, 14, and 425 pupils respectively.

In the United States, we are accustomed to school "systems" or "districts" (i.e. the Buffalo school system, or the Fayetteville school district) all run by a central administration and a school board, all responsible to the State Education Department. The international schools we are talking about — sometimes loosely referred to as the "International School System" — belong to no system or district. Each one is a solitary, independent unit which is and has to be sufficient unto itself. It is responsible to no government (except in that it must comply with all applicable governmental laws for private establishments) and to no higher authority — excepting the children it serves (which may be the highest of all). Some of these schools were begun by two or three mothers of school age children who taught their own youngsters, possibly aided by a correspondence course. Others were sponsored by church missionary groups or by companies which had assigned enough personnel to a particular locality to warrant forming a school for their children. Still others were formed by an enterprising educator who saw a need and started a school. The famous American School in London, now boasting a five million dollar modern, open-classroom, airconditioned, closed-circuit TV equipped plant and enrolling over a thousand pupils, resulted directly from Stephen L. Eckard's agreement, twenty years ago, to tutor four boys in his London apartment.

One of many shocks which greets the average American businessman as he begins his first assignment abroad is the size of the school tuition bill. If, as is frequently the case, he has three children of high school age, his bill for the three will be $4,000 in Islamabad (Pakistan), $4,200 in Kodaikanal (India), $5,340 in Jeddah (Saudi Arabia), and about $6,900 in Zurich (Switzerland). Except for the fact that his company will probably pick up the tab, one could hear him explode. And, in Belgium ($1,840 per child in secondary school in the International School of Brussels), explode he will, because the company payment of his school bill is regarded by the Belgian government as taxable salary at perhaps the 45% to 55% level.

International independent schools receive no tax support from city or state; they must be operated on tuition fees from parents. In contrast, the cost of public schooling in the United States is shared by all property owners in the school district whether they have children or not. As an example, let us look at the Joneses (no children), the Smiths (two children) and the Johnsons (six children) who own identical houses next door to each other. Each family will pay the same lump sum school tax each year — let us say, $800. Thus, the Joneses get no direct benefit and are likely to be heard muttering they are paying $800 for nothing; the Smiths are paying $400 a year in tuition for each of their two children, while it costs the Johnsons only $133 per year per child. Transfer these three families to Lima, Peru; enroll the children in the American School there, and the Joneses will pay nothing, the Smiths will pay $2,000, while the Johnsons will have to fork up $6,000. If both Smith and Johnson work for the same company and are competing with each other for the overseas assignment, it will cost the company $4,000 more to transfer Johnson rather than Smith. Should a company's business require it to send a man to a location where there is no school, it will cost the company from $4,000 to $5,000 for each child it places in a Swiss boarding school!

But let us move from finance, and consider quality. How good are these overseas schools? What quality of education will children receive in Yokahama – or Bogota – or Frankfurt?

Many a large volume has been written on what constitutes "quality" in education. There is no room here for more than an expression of my conviction as to its importance. The old expression "half a loaf is better than no bread" does not, in my opinion, apply to the education of a child – any child – unless the half-loaf in question is entirely a matter of quantity – not quality. Five or six subjects badly taught for a year can do incalcuable damage to a child, either at home or abroad, but much more so if he has been rudely and suddenly transplanted to a foreign land.

Some overseas schools have been "accredited" by one of the six U.S. accrediting associations or, in Europe, by the European Council of International Schools. Accreditation is, indeed, one measure of school quality, for it assures the public that the school in question has been formally inspected by a professional accrediting team and found to meet certain essential education standards. Such accreditation is not the only evaluative guarantee. There are a good many international schools which carry no formal accreditation, but which are easily the equal in quality, in all respects, of some of the best schools in the United States. Let us discuss, then, what we feel to be two of the prime factors affecting the quality of education of a youngster in an overseas school: the teacher and the learner.

How good is the teaching? Generally, teachers in overseas schools are excellent. During the last ten years, I have personally reviewed the credentials of approximately five thousand applicants for teaching positions abroad. In that same period, I have observed a great deal of teaching. I repeat, in general, the teaching overseas is excellent. For the most part, the teachers in American International schools abroad are very well qualified; they are young, but experienced; they are imaginative, resourceful, and devoted to kids and to teaching. They tend to be "full of beans and ideas" and they impart a vitality to the classroom and its work that is refreshing and good.

However, they don't tend to stay too long. Some go abroad for one sabbatical year; others contract for two or three years. It is the rare American who decides, at age twenty-seven, to become an expatriate and to make a career of teaching abroad.

Any good schoolmaster anywhere will agree that the quality of education offered in any school is definitely affected by the degree of permanence or length of tenure of the teaching and administrative staff. A good educational program is far more than good pupil plus good teacher plus good books and equipment. It is all that plus a sound and growing philosophy and a teamwork that grows out of a well led school staff working effectively together for years. Unfortunately, it is the rare international school in which one will find a teacher or administrator who has been there more than two or three or perhaps five years. As to overseas administrators, there is a saying that ". . . the average tenure of an international school headmaster is 2-2-2-2" — meaning two years, two months, two days, and two minutes. As this statement is being typed, I can think of one young school in southern Europe that has had three principals in its first two years — and of a twelve-year old boarding school that has had nine or ten different headmasters. Of the seventy-five teachers on the current faculty list of one large overseas school, the only names which were on the faculty list of five years ago are the ten men and women who married local people and have put down family roots.

Another problem related to turnover and thus to the quality of a school and its program is the frequency of change in the Boards of Directors of these schools. Most board members are U.S. or English business men or diplomats who change assignments with alarming frequency — alarming, that is to the school administrator who, having carefully adjusted his sights, ways, procedures, educational goals and plans to the particular notions of a majority of the Board, suddenly finds that the majority has become the minority. He either must change his sights, ways, educational goals, etc., to conform to the ideas of the new majority, or he rapidly becomes a "Joseph whom Pharaoh knoweth not." In the former case, he girds his educational loins to see out his contract and starts looking for greener pastures; in the latter case, he becomes a member of the 2-2-2-2 Society.

In mentioning the two prime factors which I feel affect the quality of education in overseas schools, I have all too briefly touched on one of them, the quality of teaching. The other is the mental and emotional health of the child who has been summarily yanked out of the school, the home, the town to which he is accustomed, and has been dropped like a parachuted package into a strange community. He finds few who speak his language or dress in a like manner. He experiences a strange climate where it may snow in July and boil at Christmastime. He finds his daily life bereft of intelligible movies, or television or radio, of hot dogs and hamburgers, of the corner drug store and other familiar haunts, his buddies, and his girl friend. And sometimes, to boot, he discovers he has lost his parents — at least partially — because they become too absorbed in new adult contacts to stay as close to their children as they are needed.

As remarked in the ECIS Directory of the European Council of International Schools: "Parents would be well advised to remember that, when they accept an overseas assignment involving a change of residence and of school for the children, *they* are moving because they want to. The children have no choice. Some children face a move and school change with anticipation and excitement; others can face it with a fear and dread which they may or may not show. The case, insight, and understanding which are handled in connection with a major move can have significant effects on the educational and personal development of the children."

Culture shock is a familiar phenomenon to all transplanted families. Some thrive on the challenge; others wilt and either suffer or go home. Some families split down the middle, with parents loving the change, novelty, and excitement — and with children hating and resenting everything — or vice versa. But however the entry occurs, unless the whole family gets over whatever degree of shock they experience, the children's success and growth in school and as people — regardless of the high quality of teaching and administration and school program — will be adversely affected.

The shock of transplantation of families overseas into a strange culture may often act as a catalyst to unleash forces within the family structure and within each family member which existed before the move. In the pattern of living "at home" there is a sense of security in all that is familiar and well known. When the cloak of familiar things and surroundings and activities is taken away, one's insecurities — if one has them — are laid bare. Retreat into dislike and fear of the new mode of life is a form of defense.

Parents whose married life "at home" is on firm ground, and whose children "at home" are secure in their family life and their knowledge of their own identities need have little fear of cutlure shock. Their move from Minneapolis to Afghanistan (and there is a fine American International School in Kabul) will be exciting, though full of adjustments for parents and children. It will have no more deleterious effect on family life or on the children's success in school than if they moved to St. Paul. On the other hand, if parents think that the move abroad will give their tottering marriage a new breath of life and a fresh start, or that it will either stop Junior's current experimenting with marijuana or will lift him out of a C-minus performance in General Math, they have another think coming. The culture shock they may experience could possible apply the *coup de grace* to their marriage and send Junior on the high road to further problems.

If it is thought that I have wandered too widely from our subject, let it be said that American International Schools overseas are very like their Stateside counterparts **except** for their impact on children and parents whose culture shock is severe and sustained. Most overseas schools are poorly equipped to handle children under such strain.

Some services to which American children and their parents are accustomed in schools at home are missing to a lesser or a greater degree overseas, depending on the size and financial health of the school. By and large, these overseas schools are good — repeat, good. There are some weak and struggling ones. But most of them rank in quality well in the upper half of schools of similar size in the United States. They are primarily academic schools. They are generally well equipped and staffed to handle and to teach well the reasonably well-adjusted, academically average or above-average child. Almost every overseas high school offers Advanced Placement courses in at least one discipline. However, most of them are not staffed to effectively handle retardates, or children who suffer from mental or emotional problems of any real severity. Herein lies one of the major differences between Stateside and overseas schools. Psychological services, remedial specialists, special adjustment classes, speech and hearing therapists, guidance counselors, full scale nursing services — are not ordinarily available. There is a very simple reason: money — or rather, lack of it. To staff a school to render well the foregoing special services in addition to the regular academic program could increase the annual tuition fee per child by $300 to $500 — or more — and more than one conscientious overseas school Headmaster who has fought to include these services in his overseas school program — because he and his teachers found they were sorely needed — landed in the 2-2-2-2 Society.

Neither are the best of overseas schools exclusively "American" in pattern and program. It is interesting to observe how some groups of parents heartily approve the internationalization of the school program, while others resent it, and frequently battle to have a school which is in Belgium become a carbon copy of a school in Denver, Colorado. There is, perhaps, a normally nationalistic conceit in Americans who so frequently "when in Rome do **not** do as the Romans do", but do everything the American way. They must show the Romans how to do things better. I do not agree with Admiral Rickover's contention that European education is better than American education. There are excellences of educational viewpoint, pattern, and practice to be found in the different systems of education in different cultures. The best of the American International Schools overseas blend into the American curriculum and teaching pattern those excellences of approach, technique, and standards of academic accomplishment from foreign systems of education that serve to enrich and improve. The introduction of the International Baccalaureate by some of these schools is but one example.

Children who are fortunate enough to spend five or more educationally fruitful years in international schools overseas — preferably the last five years before entering an American college — will, in my opinion, forever have an "edge" on their less fortunate contemporaries. If these years have been well spent — in addition to mastering at high school level the basic academic disciplines — they will speak, read, and write one or more foreign languages with almost native fluency. This alone opens doors of reading and research which remain closed to others. Their knowledge and understanding of history and the inter-relation of the nations of the world will have been enriched by having lived and observed cultures other than their own. They may have been stunned into silent contemplation by their first sight of Michaelangelo's Pieta in St. Peters – or of the Taj Mahal – or of the snow atop Fujiyama – or of the dawn coming up "like thunder out of China 'cross the bay." They will have seen the peoples of many lands, in the fields and in the market places – some naked, some hungry – some rich, overbearing, or cruel. They will have learned the priceless virtue of adaptability to things and ways that, although not American, are common to much of the rest of the world.

And if they have had eyes to see, ears to hear, minds that are searching and sensitive, and hearts to be reached, they will have learned to know and to cherish values in life far greater than unnecessarily large and powerful automobiles, frozen TV dinners, the dizzy and ulcer-creating drive to accumulate more and more of this world's material goods, and the need for flush-toilet bathrooms – at least two or three to a family.

If, in their years abroad, they have reached out and made their own all that the International Schools and their environments have offered them, they will indeed have gained what we in international education call "the extra ingredient" in their total makeup. This we believe to be essential to effective membership in today's world.

Chapter 2

THE ORIGIN AND DEVELOPMENT
OF THE DEPARTMENT OF DEFENSE OVERSEAS
DEPENDENT SCHOOLS

William G. Thomas and Thomas T. Drysdale

The rubble and the smoldering fires of World War Two are gone. Motor pools remain, as do tanks, barbed wire, reviewing stands, and military men and women. But the mood of building peace is different than that of conducting a war or helping a former enemy pick himself up from the depths of defeat.

Even as the ashes of destruction were cleared and reconstruction began, the United States and its allies changed their roles from combatants to conciliators and counselors. The war was over on all fronts. It had been won at great cost. Human lives are valuable assets.

To insure what was hoped to be a lasting peace, to aid in the restoration of dignity and self-sufficiency from the debris and devastation which the conquered had realized, was indeed a formidable task. In attempting to accomplish that task, uniformed representatives of the United States, during the past twenty-seven years, have been stationed throughout the world to protect and defend the concept of universal peace.

Though no less capable nor alert than his counterpart of over a quarter-century ago, the American serviceman or woman on military installations or aboard ships is, today, neither angry nor menacing. The modern sailor, soldier, airman and marine is better paid, better educated, and certainly more highly specialized than his predessors of the pre-World War Two era. He is more inclined to be married than single. He begins a family early in his service career. He will withstand considerable hardship to be close to his family. As a family man, he would even leave the service if his family situation were direly threatened. As yet, women military careerists have not tended to develop families in a manner similar to men in overseas situations, i.e. there have been fewer of them, they have ordinarily been young and single, and there have been limited military job opportunities for them in locations outside the continental U.S.

Shortly after WWII, a number of privileges formerly only the exclusive rights of officers were extended to enlisted men. This included permitting wives and families to accompany their military breadwinners as "dependents" in overseas assignments. A whole new Pandora's Box opened for already harassed Supply Corps men, transportation officers, and logistics specialists, among others. Military bases were to become American communities, equipped with hospitals, dental clinics, veterinary services, commissaries, post

13

exchanges, apartments and laundries. While some families resided in government quarters, others lived "on the economy" — among the local people. Yet, families meant children. Children meant schools.

Initially, small independent American community schools were established by those few parents who found themselves stationed close together. Eventually, a worldwide network evolved which now includes 200 elementary and 100 junior and senior high schools.

The transiency of the occupying forces; the impossibility of immersing American children into the educational mainstreams of French, Spanish, English, Italian, German, and Japanese and other school systems; and the necessity to provide a comprehensive education which would permit American young people to progress at a normal rate of attrition were significant factors in the establishment and maintenance of the dependent school program.

More than 1,000,000 children have been educated in American dependent schools over the past twenty-seven years. More than 25,000 teachers and administrators have been employed. Each of the American military branches has assumed the educational responsibility for a section of the world in which our servicemen are stationed: the Army — Europe, Scandanavia, North Africa, and the Middle East; the Air Force — the Pacific Area; and the Navy — the Atlantic Area. The major responsibility for the dependent schools program is centralized in the Directorate for Dependents' Education in the Pentagon, under the United States Department of Defense.

In 1946, 38 elementary schools and five high schools opened in Germany for 1,297 children under the supervision of the Dependents School Service. One hundred and sixteen teachers were employed, a few of whom have remained with the school system ever since, though at that time, certainly unaware that their tenure would last so long.

By the end of School Year 1946-47, enrollments had risen to 2,992. Nine more elementary schools had been established. In Berlin, a PTA had even been organized.

By 1949, the number of dependent schools approached one hundred, as a direct result of the overseas American forces being tripled due to a series of international crises. Such incidents helped to clarify the commitment of the United States and foreign governments to the American presence on an essential and continual basis.

In 1950, as part of its reparation obligation, the German government granted sizable financial allocations to the U.S. Forces for the construction of troop and dependent housing and for schools throughout Germany.

For the next ten years, the overseas schools realized steady, though not spectacular growth. It was in the sixties that the Dependent Schools came of age as a major American school system in its own right. In 1964, with three hundred schools on Army, Navy, and Air Force installations throughout the world, the Secretary of Defense combined the three separate systems into the Department of Defense Overseas Dependents School System.

There are now more than 200 dependent schools in Europe, North Africa, and the Middle East, with the largest number in Germany. Italy and England have a dozen or more schools, and others are located in Belgium, the Netherlands, Denmark, and Norway in the north, and Spain, Morocco, Sicily, Crete, Greece, and Turkey in the Mediteranean Area. Asmara, Ethiopia is the location of the most southern dependent school. In Asia, American dependent schools can be found in Japan, Korea, Taiwan, Okinawa, and the Philippines. There are several schools in the Atlantic and Caribbean areas — Iceland, Labrador, Newfoundland, the Azores, Bermuda, and at Guantanamo Bay, Cuba. A small number of (about 20,000) American children attend private American community or international schools, primarily due to the absence of local dependent schools.

Take a place like Augsburg, Germany. Located in picturesque and friendly Bavaria, once a rest stop on the historic Romance Road, Augsburg is where Martin Luther tacked the beginning of the Reformation on Catholic church doors. The onion-shaped cathedral Steeples; the gingerbreaded-carved porch facings; the window-bedecked rows of colorful flowers; the "lederhosen"-clad, white-haired farmer loading his horse-drawn cart; the warm, gentle, yet deeply furrowed face of a peasant woman — all are typical of this German industrial center.

It is the heart of a sunny, soft-winded day. German children are in the volksshulen (elementary school), obershulen and gymnasia (high schools) or berufsschulen (trade schools); as their parents tend to homes, survival, and their occupations.

Where are the American dependent children? Naturally, they are in school. They might as well be in Midland, Michigan or San Diego, California. They sit behind neat little desks in contoured chairs. In the front of them in their attractive classroom are an American flag on one side, a blackboard in the middle, and a schedule of the day on the other side. They are surrounded by a scattered assortment of pictures of former American presidents, maps at various heights of spring tension, and an array of last week's homework assignments. Such is the typical elementary school setting, whether in the United States or in a dependent school overseas. These educational islands of American culture are present wherever a large enough contingent of American servicemen are stationed or occasionally dock ship or plane. They exist on craggy, treeless frontiers of remoteness and in the busiest sections of the most sophisticated foreign cities of the world. American education, dependent school K-12 variety, has been the family camp follower of the modern era.

Such is the sketchy background of the United States dependent school movement. It has an enrollment of 160,000 students, kindergarten through grade twelve, in twenty-six foreign countries throughout the world. In geographical scope, it is the largest school system on earth. As a system, it employs more teachers and administrators, approximately 8,000, from all of the different states and territories of the U.S., than any other single school system. It also has a high turnover of staff and students. Three to four years is the average tenure. It is varied and complicated. Its school responsibilities range from 6,852 at Fort Buckner in the Ryuku Islands (Okinawa) to 20 in Jever, Germany.

Thus, in a little over a quarter-century, the overseas dependent school story which began in Cuba and the bombed ruins of Austria, Germany, and Japan, has unfolded in Europe, Scandinavia, the Middle East and North Africa, the Pacific and Asia. It is a story which portrays much about the cutting edge of world education and international understanding. Its leading characters are school children who represent an entire generation of American youth schooled under circumstances unique to man's history — a generation more immersed in history than any generation before them. Born in the ashes of man's most destructive conflagration, they are an integral part of youth's most universal drive toward lasting international harmony.

Students in DoD schools share much in common with their peers in the U.S., but they experience many different situations and activities as well. What do they have in common? These overseas students dress and act very much like students attending public schools in any of the fifty states. They are involved in most of the same course studies. They are concerned about grades, college, dating, drugs, student protests, dress codes, and their future careers. They have interscholastic sports, debate contests, prom nights, graduation ceremonies, and adhere to all of the traditional rituals of their imitated models at home. They have much in common with their stateside counterparts.

Dependent students also are involved in much that is different. They come from every state and territory of the United States. On the average, each of them has lived in at least one foreign country before he finishes the fourth grade. Upon graduation from high school, he will have attended at least three different schools in at least two different countries. At all age levels, they perform at a slightly higher level than the national norms in achievement and intelligence tests. Few of them are dropouts. They emphasize their educations for many reasons, among them the lack of full or part-time employment opportunities on overseas military installations. More than half of them enter colleges and universities; many pursue technical programs beyond high school in various vocationally-oriented institutions.

Even with family incomes which vary, extremities of poverty or affluence are non-existant. Additionally, the racial problems which have occured in many parts of the United States, are considerably more severe than those found in the racially-integrated dependent school system. Many mothers, and some children, have become Americans after first being citizens of another nation; they may speak one or more languages other than English.

There are other dissimilarities, which overseas American dependent youth may take for granted. Milk is delivered by airplane, rather than by truck, to remote Pacific Islands. The local shopping mall is usually a military post exchange run by a monopoly. The commanding officer of a military installation is the "mayor" and direct representative of the U.S. Secretary of Defense rolled into one. There are always two police forces, the native one off base and the military one on base. Life in the United States is translated by the *Army Times*, the Armed Forces Radio/Television Network, and the last arrival from CONUS (Continental United States).

High school and elementary school groups ski the Zugspitze; an athletic team from Munich can relax among the wonders of the Dahlem Museum before a ball game with Berlin High School; there are long excursions to Paris, Athens, Rome, Tokyo, Manilla, and other renowned cultural centers.

These dependent young people indeed live on the edge of history – in view of the Berlin Wall, the China Sea, and within earshot of the 6-Day War. They play near international military and political headquarters visited by the world's leaders, by Presidents, Prime Ministers, Royalty, and Ambassadors. They study in the shadows of historic castles, battlegrounds, and landmarks. At various times, they have been evacuated from Pakistan, Turkey, Libya, and Cuba; and removed, in massive political actions, from France and Austria.

What of the teachers? Like their students, they represent every state and territory of the U.S. They combine a high ratio of experience (an average of ten years) and preparation (thirty-one percent have graduate degrees), with comparative youth (an average age of thirty-nine). More than seventy percent of all DoD teachers are female; about 43% are married. More than 60% have served less than three years.

Ordinarily, they adjust well to a variety of living and working conditions. They adapt satisfactorily to patterns of culture which are new and strange to them. They benefit from the perspective of viewing the American education system from abroad and from working closely with teachers and students who come from many parts of the United States.

Teachers are given considerable freedom to experiment and innovate, while following a relatively standardized curriculum. They accept and help to make meaningful change.

What about the curriculum? The educational programs of DoD schools are patterned on the offerings of the best public elementary and secondary schools in the United States. All 58 DoD high schools are fully accredited by the North Central Accrediting Association.

Each overseas location also provides exceptionally rich opportunities to supplement study with experiences derived from two unique environmental sources – the military community and the host nation community. The military establishment employs a broad spectrum of specialists and supports numerous activities, particularly in the technological and scientific fields. These specialists and activities enrich the local educational program as do linguistics and inter-cultural opportunities which are developed from host nation resources. There is instruction in over fifteen different foreign languages. Teachers first designed courses in the Romance Languages and German, and later used them as models for the study of Turkish, Danish, Norwegian, Amharic, Arabic, Chinese, Japanese, and Tagalog.

Many overseas schools are literally laboratories of intercultural education. Their locations make it possible; commitment makes it happen. It is not confined to one teacher or to one class period. It continues throughout the day, in language arts, in social studies, in science, in art and music. The educational programs are as inter-disciplinary as the life around and within the school. It is the study of life itself.

Additionally, there are ample opportunities for American children to live, play, and study with children of other nations. Thousands of elementary school children, accompanied by classroom teachers and parent chaperones, participate in week-long, outdoor camp-study programs. Hundreds of American children ski on the slopes of southern Bavaria, northern Italy, and Japan. Often, they accompany children of host nations. Together, they tour ancient castles and cathedrals, attend concerts, international student forums, folkfests, and sports events. In some locations, children of various countries live in youth hostels for a week or two, playing and working together, and, above all, forming lasting friendships.

A culturally enriched educational program is the commitment of Dr. M. Richard Rose, Deputy Assistant Secretary of Defense for Education. Current objectives which have been established for the DoD overseas schools include:

- Increasing career and vocational education for all students — K-12.

- Exploring ways in which the school calendar can better suit the needs of military families overseas.

- Investigating the concept of the utilization of outstanding teachers half-time as Master Teachers to assist others and coordinate subject areas vertically.

- Establishing developmental reading programs for all junior and senior high school students regardless of their reading abilities.

- Studying ways in which the discretionary use of free or leisure time can be taught at all grade levels along with career education.

There is also much attention given to providing pupil personnel services to supplement and complement the educational program. Special education classes are conducted for mentally retarded, those with learning disabilities, and pre-school handicapped, blind, deaf, orthopedically handicapped and emotionally disturbed children.

Home instruction courses are available for a small number of students living in remote areas where there are no military school facilities and for the physically handicapped who cannot attend school. Isolated children in grades 1 through 8 study under the Calvert system. Isolated high school students who elect not to attend a dependent dormitory school follow the University of Nebraska correspondence courses.

Speech and remedial reading specialists are assigned to larger school complexes or district offices to assist teachers in improving student communication skills.

School social workers interpret child and family problems to teachers and counselors and perform valuable liaison service with medical clinics and local community resources. Psychologists frequently visit smaller schools to test children who are referred for special help.

The "live-in" or dormitory schools located in numerous countries are staffed with counselors who provide supervision and scholastic and academic advisement.

Additionally, most schools have nurses assigned to them on a full-time basis. Their primary responsibilities are to provide health education services and to oversee activities related to emergency care for illness and accidents, screening for hearing and vision problems, establishing policy and surveillance practices concerning communicable diseases and student physical examinations.

Now, what of present circumstances? As this paper is written, we are not at war. We are no longer drafting young men into the military. As a matter of fact, militarism has been de-emphasized. Our armed forces are to be voluntary, rather than mandated organizations. The value and necessity of and for our far-flung outposts of uniformed support of Asian and European countries is being emphatically questioned. The "Cold War" has warmed. We have inflationary conditions in the United States. There have been changes in military strategies and technologies. Many of our nation's domestic problems require immediate attention and resolution. The threat of war and the spread of communism no longer loom as lightening bolts on the horizon. Times, and factors which greatly affect the United States dependent school program, have changed radically.

In closing this chapter, we have asked several questions which may have passed through the minds of readers as to the future direction of the dependent school movement:

How will dependent schools be affected by the possible reduction of troops throughout the world? If there is a reduction of American servicemen abroad, most assuredly there will be a comparable decrease in the number of dependents and schools which serve dependent children. The dependent schools will continue to have the responsibility to fulfill the needs of the children of DoD military and civilian personnel.

What type of dependent school program will exist with voluntary military forces? Probably, the nature of the program will be the same as it has been; presumably, with even greater flexibility.

Will military installations be more spread out geographically? Will they be large or small? At present, these are impossible questions to answer. It might be assumed that with the United States' portrayal as more of a peacemaker in changing from a military alert status to a monitoring system, we will have more "firewatch" stations and fewer "firehouse" stations. Our military installations could be in strategic and more geographically distant locations from one another. Some would be large; others small. It would depend on the responsibilities and the work to be accomplished.

If both "hot" and "cold" wars are absent, will we have more "soldier-diplomats" serving in the military overseas, i.e. individuals who are familiar with the language of the host country, its customs, and who have special educations and skills, etc.? This would be most desirable and not impossible. Who knows if it will be a reality?

Will there be more assimilation of military people and dependents into foreign cultures? It will probably be heightened in emphasis as the climate becomes friendlier.

The exact direction of what has been often described as "the most uniuqe school system in the world" is cloudy, even as the international policies of our nation which so affect the system are uncertain, undetermined and affected so greatly by conditions and changes throughout the world. In looking back, the story of the dependent schools is a successful one; one which is proven daily by the contributions and performances of its hundreds of thousands of alumni and thousands of current students. In looking forward, history is probably our best predictor. Besides, how many American children can boast, as did the small offspring to his Army sergeant father stationed in Germany:

"Daddy, ya'know what? A chim'ny sweep vis'td our class today!"

Chapter 3

REFLECTIONS ON OVERSEAS STUDY PROGRAMS*

William F. Sturner

A recent evaluation of Oakland University's overseas study program convinced us of the efficacy of a simple and thus unusual approach. It dawned on us, after attending conferences, reading papers and articles, and studying models used by other institutions, that the best approach to assessing undergraduate overseas study programs demanded less research on the unique and the obscure and more reflection on the obvious. New interpretations and dramatic orientations were not vital or even necessary: what we needed was a consistent application to overseas projects of the standards which permeated our own academic programs. How to attain quality control, to realize maximum potential, to build a linkage between conceptual and experiential knowledge, to activate an awareness of the new and a reflection on the old culture, and to prepare for sophisticated study programs through the successful completion of prerequisites were the central themes that we had to analyze and implement.

This approach and the philosophical and practical conclusions it produced may not be particularly significant to institutions with many years of experience in this field — although I am reminded of a comment by the director of one of the oldest and largest university overseas programs in America who in response to my query last year confessed: "I am never quite sure that we really know what we are doing and why." But our recently acquired perspective may offer some specific clues and heuristic insights to institutions like ours which have sponsored only a few programs over the last several years and are now anxious to rethink the methods and the modes of that commitment in the hope of fully realizing its potential.

Both honesty and symmetry demand that I present a general philosophy of overseas education experiences before recommending particular types of programs or specific methods of implementation. Without the standards that emerge from a discussion of goals one cannot meaningfully or systematically propose concrete approaches to the many facets of such programs, or hope to convince others of their merit. Thus in the interests of posing acceptable particulars, I focus first on the broader question of objectives. Many of the ideas here expressed are certainly not new; I was aware of the existence of professional opinions and I pay suitable homage to their insights by borrowing from them accordingly. The synthesis, however, is mine and I hide not behind the counsel of those whose wisdom guided its formation. The result is one man's and one institution's estimate as to what represents an effective and successful educational experience in a foreign setting. Perhaps

*This article is reprinted with permission. It appeared in the 1970 fall issue of International Educational *Exchange* magazine.

these reactions will generate moves to gather the data to confirm or modify its recommendations. In the meantime, it is hoped that this will raise enough issues to be the catalyst of its own perfection.

Different overseas programs, emphasizing different subjects for different audiences, naturally have different goals. A project tailored to the needs of majors in Slavic language and literature will stress language proficiency in the context of cultural contact; programs in international relations for upperclassmen invariably will emphasize in-depth analysis by university and local experts and first-hand exposure to contemporary political problems; those interested primarily in general education have a wider range of relevant subjects from which to choose, the selections being determined by the degree to which the courses can build on the cultural setting in which the program is offered.

Whatever the department or clientele, the goal should be to maximize the efficacy of formal schooling by actual experience in and of the culture. Despite the more closely defined and structured objectives of the language and other departmental majors, such programs should not, and need never be abstracted from the virtues of the general education experience. The opportunities for cross-cultural understanding and communication, the discovery of otherness and the self and cultural examination it produces, the accent on cultural immersion and the attendant development of new emphathies and identities − these are what make studying in a foreign setting different from studying on the home campus.

To travel a thousand miles to accomplish what could be readily obtained at home, at less expense, is foolish. Similarly, the stay in a foreign culture is wasted if the student does not realize the potential to build on conceptual knowledge and simultaneously integrate it with the multifaceted aspects of cultural assimilation.

Language and Culture

Dr. Irwin Abrams of Antioch College captured the philosophy of studying abroad in an address before the National Association for Foreign Student Affairs in 1967. "Study French?" he asked. "That can be done at home. But study the French? That's something else again. It is now a new subject matter our students are seeking to master abroad; it is a new culture." Note, of course, that studying the French does not preclude the study of French, because some knowledge of the language is often a prerequisite for, and a result of cultural contact. Participating in a new culture invariably deepens interests and progress in academic disciplines including language proficiency. Whatever the specific subjects studied, the total cultural experience inevitably engulfs them.

It must be emphasized, then, that course work and cultural contact reinforce one another, and each has a way of accenting the virtues of the other. It should also be noted that it is wrong to assume that mere visual exposure will produce cultural understanding through osmosis. Proximity to the physical aspects of society is not a qualitative substitute for vigorous training in formal course work related to the culture, or an acceptable replacement for more substantive activities associated with experiencing a foreign culture. To lose sight of the fact that a university-sponsored program is intended to be a substantive academic-experiential program is to fall prey to the temptation to be mesmerized by the mere newness of the surroundings or the excitement of visual contact, no matter how superficial. The objective of a university program is to produce quality learning both within the classroom and through meaningful and purposeful cultural assimilation.

Obviously study abroad differs radically from travel abroad. The fact that a university is the sponsoring agency, and that the participants are faculty members and students, by definition means that the project has goals that differ from, or at least go beyond, the objectives of tourism. The accent in university programs must necessarily be on quality education and on both conceptual and experiential understanding of the foundations and contemporary workings of a different culture.

The tourist, on the other hand, because of his frantic pace and his expansive itinerary, emphasizes a dispersed and fragmented visual exposure to the famous landmarks of the society. He thus is often unable to experience, no less recognize, the goals of cultural understanding and the development of empathy with the new and reflection on the old culture that are central to university-sponsored overseas experiences. Students who wish to tour should be referred to tourist agencies. Students who seek courses that can be studied just as well or better in the home setting should be counseled to stay on campus. Those who wish to seize on the unique opportunity to complement conceptual knowledge in a given area or subject with first-hand in-depth experience of the culture and society upon which the academic study depends or is an outgrowth are those equipped with the proper mental and psychological outlook to benefit from study projects in foreign cultures.

Preparation Required

Since it is the duty and responsibility of the university to produce quality learning, the administrators and faculty must emphasize the same degree of concern about quality in overseas study as they do about instruction offered on the campus. Here the question of prerequisites is central. To study advanced physics one must first successfully complete basic courses in mathematics as well as physics.

The issue is no different in foreign study programs. To live in, communicate with, and absorb a foreign culture without at least some

elementary knowledge of the native culture defeats the concept of prerequisites so essential to education at the home campus. In the judgment of
some, there are circumstances in which training in the language prior to
arrival is not necessary because a student normally is able to grasp the
language quickly if he lives with a family or is placed in similar circumstances
which closely approximate physical and mental immersion in the culture.
There are several programs in existence which make this assumption,
including the University of Arizona's Center in Guadalajara, Mexico;
Professor Rocco Linsalata's Escuola de Vicenza in Italy; and certain programs
offered through the Experiment in International Living in Putney, Vermont.

Even the programs that assume that lack of knowledge of the language is
not a barrier to cultural contact, if in fact true contact commences soon after
arrival, require a grounding in the culture – customs, politics, history, art,
music – of the area, gained either through special orientation or formal
courses. Argentina or India are as foreign to the average American student as
is chemistry or biology to the average student of the humanities or social
sciences. One must become familiar with at least the basic culture of that
which is otherwise foreign before one can study, absorb, or communicate
with the area.

Southeast Asia and chemistry are thus in the same category as far as the
untutored is concerned. To thrust a student suddenly into the center of
Vienna without at least some facility in the language – or the means of
quickly attaining it by living with a family – and a grounding in the culture
of the city and the Austrian society, is closely akin to allowing a student to
take advanced physics without the proper training in mathematics and
successful completion of elementary and intermediate level physics. The
unprepared could make some progress, once loneliness and frustration were
replaced with determination, but no amount of will power exercised in a
single semester can overcome the deficiences which only directed training can
rectify. More importantly, the unprepared student cannot tap the full
potential of such sophisticated endeavors as study abroad or advanced
physics. He will learn something, he will attain some minimal goals, he will
survive, and he will boast of all three; but he will not be able to seize upon
the opportunities afforded by preparation, or achieve the optimal benefits
inherent in such sophisticated learning programs.

Such difficulties are usually complicated by the fact that the average
student has but 13 to 15 short weeks in the foreign setting, many of which
must be spent acquiring the basic information and rudimentary tools of
communication which could or should have been obtained before he arrived.
Many students will surely return to a foreign setting later in life as a tourist,
but few will have another opportunity to spend an entire semester studying
and absorbing a culture different from their own. In short, the benefits
derived are usually commensurate with the level of preparation.

Careful Planning

For the reasons already stated, and because of the particular standards outlined later in this discussion, it is strongly recommended that both the objectives of future study abroad programs and the specific method of implementation be clearly stated and explained by the sponsoring faculty (project directors) or departments and that such directors present visible evidence of planning at each stage of internal review. Such procedures are necessary because each program creates, in essence, a new set of educational experiences, almost a unique interdisciplinary concentration. Thus the university must not be reluctant to ask the sponsors to justify the program, in general and in specific, just as it requires comparable projects on the home campus to run the gamut of relevant chairmen, deans, and university curriculum committees. It is not suggested that these programs fit a set mold; this review procedure should display the same faith in the integrity and expertise of the faculty as is the case with domestic programs. But it is recommended that each prospective program, however individually stylized, be examined by persons other than the sponsors and assessed according to broad guideline standards similar to those underlined here.

Some may view overseas study programs as simply extensions of courses offered domestically and therefore immune from review and evaluation. But overseas programs are more than single courses or conglomerates of courses; they usually represent new ad hoc interdisciplinary concentrations which creatively blend curricular and cocurricular activities. Such hybrids are not in the same category as individual courses offered by individual instructors, nor are they the product of entirely new disciplines or departments. Individual courses may not be evaluated systematically (although they may be informally), whereas the process of approval for new disciplines can be a long and arduous process. Programs to study abroad occupy a middle ground and, as unique syntheses should be systematically reviewed by a faculty committee on overseas study programs, as well as by the departments and colleges affected.

Important Considerations

What then are the specific types of prerequisites, quality controls, and living-learning arrangements which would allow a university to offer interested students a high quality program of study abroad? What types of programs would most effectively generate cultural contact and all its attendant learning experiences?

Selection of Faculty
The faculty member who accompanies or leads groups of students on

overseas study programs should, of course, know the language well enough to coordinate effectively the curricular and cocurricular activities of the program. Similarly he should be steeped in some aspects of the culture of the area and be able to conduct, with the assistance of others if need be, formal and informal orientation programs for the students before and during their stay; courses on the history, politics, sociology, or other aspects of the foreign culture while abroad; and integrative summary reflections on the experience of studying abroad at the time of re-entry.

Given these credentials, the best man is usually the man who strongly desires to participate in such programs. The selection process ideally would be one in which the university accepted the enthusiastic initiative of the faculty member; it would not activate or create his interest but respond to it and baptize it by name. The gratifications of teaching abroad are not without considerable responsibilities, and the job is often time-consuming and arduous. Those instructors concerned only with teaching and researching can and surely will resist engagement in the extracurricular aspects of the program. Warm bodies recruited to staff the program would normally approach the project with a greater degree of egocentrism, less dedication to the objectives of the program, and less sustained interest in the cocurricular and cultural contact needs of the students.

The staffing of the program should be approved, at every stage of planning, by the relevant chairmen and deans to keep tabs on the financial obligations the departments and the university are likely to incur and to minimize dislocations in staffing caused by the absence of many instructors, or those whose specialty is particularly needed on campus in a given semester. Inadequate clearance can mean that the interested faculty members jeopardize their chances of going abroad or cause serious deficiences on the campus for the duration of their absence, deficiencies that can be filled only by hiring interim personnel at great additional expense. The responsibility for obtaining clearance should, of course, rest with the prospective faculty participant. In fact, a formal application procedure by which the faculty member outlines the details of his proposal might very well be forwarded successively to all concerned parties with the aid of a cover-sheet to facilitate routing, comments, and signatures of approval.

Selection of Students

Overseas study programs must be considered special programs for which the students must qualify. The right to participate must be earned through successful completion of certain prerequisites. Although the faculty and staff involved will be best able to define the particular standards necessary under the special circumstances, there are minimal standards which could apply to every program: (1) sophomore standing or above; (2) good academic standing; (3) social and psychological fitness; and (4) successful completion of courses or an orientation program in prescribed aspects of the culture of the area.

Since one of the primary goals of such programs is to engender cross-cultural understanding and reflection on the values and activities of the parent culture as well as the new one, it is not unreasonable to limit the programs to those who have completed at least one year of college. The recommendation is based on the assumption that sophomores as a class, relative to freshmen, possess a greater degree of general maturity and a deeper understanding of their own culture, factors essential to an effective experience of otherness. To allow freshmen to join overseas study programs might also aggravate the confusion and lack of direction which often characterize the first year in college. Some programs may wish to limit the program to juniors or first semester seniors, depending on the standards set regarding language proficiency, cultural-orientation prerequisites, and major department qualifications.

Regarding general academic performance, it is taken for granted that every program will require the participating students to be in good academic standing (i.e., a minimum of a C average). Some faculty members or departments may require at least a C+ average under the assumption that this would help minimize the number of sluggards and lark-seekers. This is understandable in view of the fact that the faculty-student relationship while abroad is inevitably very close and continuous; students who have academic or social problems can be quite disruptive to the group and most frustrating and annoying for the instructor. Students and faculty abroad cannot escape from such problems after 3 p.m. or on weekends but are wedded to them every minute of the day for the duration of the program.

Several researchers are currently devising procedures for the systematic testing and interviewing of students and faculty for adaptability to, and attitudes toward, living in a foreign culture, and several procedures of varying degrees of sophistication are being used at several universities. Because of questions as to the effectiveness of such testing — at least in the minds of some — and the political problems incurred in testing the psychological fitness of students, no less faculty, it is often advisable to institute a formal application and review procedure. In addition to a written application (noting how the student qualified according to grades, academic progress, and completion of prescribed prerequisites), the students should be requested to submit at least two letters of evaluation from faculty members assessing the student's academic potential, dependability and social characteristics. A committee of review should also check with the office of the dean of students for any information that would counsel against the student's inclusion in such a program. These are, of course, delicate matters, but the effectiveness of the program — both for the individual students and for the group — may very well depend on screening out those who are highly unlikely to survive in a foreign culture, or whose records indicate they might have a seriously detrimental effect on the other students or might in any number of ways jeopardize the success of the program. Such review procedures should exist, with or without formal psychological testing, to minimize risk and maximize the potential success of what is, after all, a group project of limited duration, in a foreign culture, with a whole set of unique social and political pressures for the students, the faculty, the sponsoring university, and the host country.

Sponsoring faculty and departments must assume responsibility for noting prescribed courses in the regular curriculum and/or conducting ad hoc orientation programs during the several weeks prior to departure. Such advance information will minimize cultural shock and frustration and facilitate more rapid involvement, absorption, and assimilation. The courses and/or orientations preferably should expose the students to the social, political, and religious mores and customs of the area, and provide both the historical context and a survey of contemporary issues of the society. Orientation sessions upon re-entry to the American culture are also recommended; some students overidentify with the host culture while most become members of a third culture, a blending of both old attachments and new values. In either case, debriefing sessions that emphasize sharing experiences in reflective dialog help instill a sense of direction in re-entering the parent culture. The student thus does not leave the overseas experience feeling uprooted but attains some sense of community and continuity.

Most institutions involved in overseas study programs also insist on at least two semesters of language training, on the assumption that the language is the essential tool for understanding the culture. Others, however, insist that learning the language should more properly be a product of cultural contact which can be easily attained if the student lives with a family or undergoes a similar immersion in the culture of the host country. The choice apparently depends on the circumstances and the area of the world. In some countries language skills are required prior to arrival for psychic and educational survival, while in other areas the English language is so prevalent that knowledge of the foreign language is not crucial. There are also many opportunities for living with families who speak English, in which case proficiency in the foreign language may not be essential. In short, the language qualification for each program ought to be determined individually and only after completing both an evaluation of the particular circumstances in the area selected and an assessment of how knowledge of the language would serve the specified objectives of the program.

Living Accommodations and Cross-Cultural Encounters

Most of the problems associated with the goal of "cultural immersion" evaporate if students live with families in the host country. Opportunities to do so exist in most countries and in most areas of the world. The alternatives of pensions, villas, hotels, or other arrangements that often develop into geographic and psychological enclaves should be used only when living with families is not possible. In that case the program director must develop cocurricular activities that accent firsthand exposure to the daily living experiences of the host country. Cross-cultural contact is an inevitable consequence of living with a family, but it must be consciously arranged for instances where the living accommodations result in dependence on American friends and American customs.

Among others, the Experiment in International Living will arrange placement with families and also provide a coordinator who will reside in the area and visit with the students and families, assess their mutual progress, and arrange a series of excursions and experiences which the limited budget of the students and families do not allow. The Experiment can also provide thorough language training and orientation before departure and often en route, if transportation is via ship.

Academic Structure

There are apparently as many models as there are programs. Some use no campus faculty members but through the efforts of a campus coordinator arrange to attach the students to a local university, or hire moonlighting instructors or free-lance part-timers. Others require that the students attend local language institutes, live with families, and complete independent study or keep a diary-journal. Every gradation imaginable appears to exist, from a combination of campus and native instructors to programs manned entirely by the regular faculty of the sponsoring university.

Normally the programs most costly for the sponsoring university (computing direct and indirect costs) are those that use their own instructors to staff the program. Less costly but also considered least effectual – at least in the minds of many – are those programs that send the students to a local university or language institute or rely exclusively on hired local personnel. In these cases, the result is frequently an uncoordinated, nonintegrated, and somewhat disjointed academic program. The inundation of university towns with visiting students often produces courses for "the masses" and other characteristics associated with instructing many transient students in a relatively short period of time. This certainly is not always the case, but it has been the experience of many. In addition, if he is to qualify for "freshman" courses in the average European university, the American student usually must have completed at least two years of college, which means that American participants must be at least juniors. Instruction is also normally in the native tongue, for which many students are not adequately prepared.

The problems are compounded if the students live in the university dormitories with other Americans who just happen to converge at the same time. The result can be a frustrating experience to the student who misses a coordinated academic program, the experience of living with a family, and the series of cocurricular activities to establish cultural contact. Much of the time is spent in building some sense of belonging, which because of the circumstances usually consists more of social contacts than true cultural understanding. The hiring of local personnel can also be risky business. It is not uncommon, I am told, for even noted universities to have two faculties, one for the regular student body and another for the transient American tourist. The use of one's own faculty, then, makes for the best academic and cocurricular program abroad, but that faculty must be used effectively. One could not justify, for example, sending four faculty members, each to teach only one course, for a group of 50 students — a total credit offering of 12 to 16 credits. A reasonable ratio seems to be one faculty member for approximately every 30 students.

The instructor might offer two courses — for three to four credits each — and coordinate an independent study program — anything from research to keeping a journal — for another two to four credits. The fourth course could consist of advanced language training by a local instructor. This arrangement assumes that the students all are placed with families in the area and come together only for classes and seminars. The instructor would not have to create and coordinate a series of activities seeking to inculcate cultural understanding because such experiences would be a natural outgrowth of the family environment. Similarly, he would not have to spend time acting as resident dean of students or as the social and psychological referent point because the families absorb these functions, aided perhaps by a local resident coordinator provided or hired by the university.

If placement with families is difficult, impossible, or simply not desirable, then the instructor must assume responsibility for organizing a program of cultural activities and making himself available for informal counseling if the need arises. Such responsibilities would take the place of one formal course, the instructor then offering only one course, coordinating the independent study facet of the program, plus assuming responsibility for organizaing the cocurricular activities. An additional language course could still be staffed by local personnel.

The combination of formal course work (either one or two courses), independent study, and advanced training in the language is a good one. It meshes conceptual knowledge, reflection on experiential learning, and progress in acquiring the tool for the assimilation of the culture. In any case, the formal courses, and the projects, research, or reflection completed through independent study, should all take advantage of the opportunity to focus directly on one or another aspect of the native culture.

Types of Programs
Several persons active in overseas study programs over the years have of late cautioned against the proliferation of individual programs, many of

which duplicate existing programs sponsored by other universities. Why start a new program, or a series of them, if programs fitting the desired approach already exist? Why not cooperate with other universities or one of the many organizations that already offer a wide range of alternative programs? If this reasoning is correct, then a university that as yet has no systematic program for overseas study should evaluate its reasons for wanting to sponsor yet another venture to the already overpopulated university towns of the world.

It seems that a university would not be guilty of needless proliferation or vulnerable to the charge of self-aggrandizement if its efforts were motivated by a desire to offer programs that could become part of an integrated experience for its students and serve as an outlet for the research or general education needs of its own faculty. Students who go abroad to study after having planned for the experience through formal or cocurricular training in the culture and language of the area to be visited, and who continue to relate to that living-learning experience through courses and/or cocurricular activities after they return to campus, will obtain a totally integrated experience. Attaching oneself to the program of another institution for the isolated period of one semester is, in comparison, a compartmentalized exposure.

The integrated experience is also an investment in community-building, for it creates a coterie of individuals on campus who relate to each other through the common experiences of preparatory training, cross-cultural understanding, and the continuing interest in courses and activities related to the theme of international education. Similarly, the campus benefits from the experience of faculty members who have led or accompanied student groups overseas. The faculty member becomes one of the focal points for the continuing discussion of, and reflection on, the overseas experience by those who studied with him, all of which is, in turn, re-invested into the life of the campus as it permeates the lectures, discussions, and research of both faculty members and students. This multiplier effect can be extremely stimulating; if enough students and faculty members participate over a period of years, the liberalizing experience can influence the tone and tempo of campus life and actually minimize parochialism by building a broad intellectual outlook and a genuine awareness of otherness.

There are also many advantages to structuring permanent centers in a particular section or sections of the world, preferably one not already inundated with existing programs (like Western Europe). A variety of programs, in which the locale changes frequently or every year, is certainly justified if the programs are consonant with the needs and wishes of the department and faculty, but they do not facilitate the growth of cumulative experiences with, or the building of academic and financial contacts in, a particular area. Such accumulations make it easier to plan and perfect the program every year, and build a wider community of students who relate to similar – although not the same – experiences of living in a particular country or area.

Evaluations of the Programs

Faculty members returning from overseas study programs should file a report which evaluates the success of the program. The students should also be required to participate in formal and informal evaluation procedures. Both steps would help complete the documentation of the program and permit the university to gather the data needed to assess and perfect both the structure and the location of recommended programs, and the recruitment and selection of faculty and students. Several students, trained in social science techniques, might perhaps collect and analyze such data as their project in independent study, an enterprise which is certain to benefit both the students and the university.

Administrative Coordination

As the number of programs for overseas study sponsored by any university multiplies, the task of completing arrangements grows more arduous. Each time there is a new program, a new set of faculty and administrators repeat the same type of planning completed for the program before, going through the same time-consuming and inefficient method of start and stop, trial and error, and doing everything from scratch. The appointment of a Director of Overseas Study Programs would obviate such needless duplication and flailing about, and free the departments and faculty participants from the difficult tasks of arranging living accommodations, transportation, the hiring of local instructors if necessary, obtaining parental permission for each student, collecting fees, and other such details.

The presence of a director would also save the university a good deal of time and money otherwise spent on useless duplication, and permit the students to obtain the discounts for room, board, and transportation which are in good part forfeited when arrangements are handled through travel agencies. The university might assess the students a certain percentage of the total cost or a set fee for administrative costs. The student will still save money in the long run because the total price obtained by the director would be considerably lower than the best group rates obtained through travel agencies, and the surcharge would help defray the expenses associated with the director's office.

Faculty Review

A permanent Committee on Overseas Study Programs, advisory to the proper academic officer, should be formed to review the proposals of faculty and departments for study abroad. The committee could act as a check for quality control and adopt certain minimal standards for such programs while allowing the faculty sponsoring an overseas project a good deal of latitude in defining the objective of the program and the method of implementation.

The number of programs for overseas study, if we extrapolate from the trend of the last few years at many universities, compounded by the rapid growth rate of those institutions, is bound to increase. Without some point of review, without a committee to raise the questions posed in this discussion, without a responsible body requesting and compiling documentation concerning intent and accomplishment, chances are that the programs will proliferate without direction or knowledge of chairmen, deans, and students, and conceivably leave the university open to sponsoring student participation in programs whose quality could otherwise have been greatly enhanced.

The committee might be composed of five members: the chairman or member of the modern language department, the chairman or a member of the area studies program, a representative of the relevant academic administrator, and two faculty members experienced in overseas study programs or learned in the fields of international relations or foreign cultures. The Director of Overseas Study Programs should also sit on the committee as an ex-officio member.

Programs for study abroad are often initiated — as is also true for many other projects — with the assumption that they are valuable additions to the academic program, offering both students and faculty viable alternatives to on-campus programs, and enhancing the cosmopolitan quality of campus life. Few would argue with these conclusions or ambitions, but there could be reason to question the method by which we arrive at them. If they are simply accepted as eternal verities or supported only by the process of rationalization, then we deprive ourselves of the understanding and sense of direction that accrues from pondering and researching the goals, the methods, and the consequences of such decisions. In other words, it could be assumed — without adequate evidence and reflection — that the overseas study component is a valuable addition to the curriculum, and each successive project a necessary supplement to the existing programs. If such assumptions are supported more by bombast than reason, more rhetoric than reality — then it becomes easy to stress simply the existence of programs without concern for their effectiveness, to prefer proliferation and larger groups to the more cautious approach of smaller units capable of a greater degree of quality control, and to opt for untrammeled individualism by the sponsoring faculty and departments over the need to study, coordinate, and evaluate.

This discussion has attempted to ponder some of the first principles that usually form the basis for overseas study programs, and in so doing to assess the particular methods for implementing those assumptions. Thus the suggestions of this article are neither clever nor dramatic but they may be useful. They certainly are not new but their combination and integration may help to emphasize the obvious and clarify the assumed.

Chapter 4

U.S. OFFICE OF EDUCATION PROGRAMS ABROAD*

Robert Leetsma

The increasingly interdependent nature of the modern world places a heavy burden on the educational systems of all nations to reduce ethnocentrism. It is clear that American education is beginning to rise to the challenge at an accelerating rate. At all levels of instruction there is a growing interest in learning more about the other nations and peoples with whom we share this fragile planet.

Many Federal agencies are involved in one way or another in assisting American education in this effort. Of special significance is the contribution of the U.S. Office of Education (OE), Department of Health, Education, and Welfare (HEW), which sponsors and funds a wide variety of programs concerned with international education. Most of these programs take place in the United States, but some are carried out abroad. This article summarizes OE program activities and opportunities abroad.

Brief History of Program Development

The initial kind of activity in which the Office of Education engaged abroad was comparative education — the study of educational systems and practices active today in other countries. The various country studies published by OE are widely used not only in the professional study of comparative education but also as basic references for helping U.S. admissions officers determine the equivalence of foreign educational credentials.

The first program concerned with sending educators abroad for direct professional experience in another culture was Teacher Exchange. This program has been carried out in cooperation with the Department of State and on State Department funds since 1946.

The more sizable program efforts of today date back to 1958 when Congress, under the stimulus of sputnik, passed the National Defense Education Act (NDEA), one section of which (Title VI) authorized Federal assistance to foreign language and area studies. Given the origin of NDEA, the Office of Education was at first understandably concerned primarily with the preparation of specialists on the non-Western world. The NDEA program was and is concentrated mainly in the United States, but when appropriations under the Fulbright-Hays and Public Law 480 legislative authorities became available to the OE international programs in 1964 and 1966 respectively, a companion program effort was developed abroad.

With the cumulative achievements over time of the various programs for specialists funded under these three legislative authorities (excluding Teacher

*This article is reprinted with permission. It appeared in the 1972 fall issue of International Educational and Cultural *Exchange* magazine.

Exchange), particularly NDEA Title VI whose total appropriation to date is approximately 6 times larger than the other two combined – and especially since the establishment of the Institute of International Studies (IIS) in 1968 – the OE concern has steadily broadened to include increasing attention to the international dimensions of general education at the elementary, secondary, and undergraduate college levels. While in budgetary terms the core of the NDEA Title VI program on American campuses continues to be appropriately concentrated on the preparation of specialists, the Office of Education is now concerned with educators and educational institutions at all levels, not just the specialized graduate level.

Legislative Authority and Program Size

With the exception of the Teacher Exchange Program, which is conducted with funds transferred to OE from the State Department Fulbright-Hays appropriation, the OE overseas programs are carried out with funds appropriated by the Congress directly to the Office of Education. The legislative authorities primarily involved are the Mutual Education and Cultural Exchange Act of 1961 (the Fulbright-Hays Act) and the Agricultural Trade Development and Assistance Act of 1954, as amended (Public Law 83-480), under which U.S.-owned excess foreign currencies can be made available for educational and other purposes. Virtually all of the funds under these two appropriations are used abroad, with the sole exception of a small amount of the Fulbright-Hays dollars for the OE Foreign Curriculum Consultant Program. This program brings educators from other countries to the United States to assist American educational institutions in strengthening their programs in foreign languages, area studies, and world affairs.

While not large in total budgetary terms ($4,404,000 in Fiscal Year 1972, of which $3,268,000 was in U.S.-owned excess foreign currencies), the overseas programs of the Office of Education funded from these two appropriations constitute an important part of the total Federal effort in international education. The various OE programs are administered in an integrated fashion by the Institute of International Studies (IIS), the bureau primarily responsible for the Office of Education's wide range of international concerns and activities.

The large proportion of the total that is in the form of U.S.-owned excess foreign currencies inevitably limits the bulk of current program activity, particularly for group projects, to a relatively small number of countries. The countries most frequently so involved in recent years have been India, Poland, Egypt, Yugoslavia, Tunisia, and Morocco. The OE program activities in other countries are funded with dollars appropriated to the Office of Education under Section 102(b)(6) of the Fulbright-Hays Act. This section of the act provides for the promotion of foreign language and area studies in American schools, colleges, and universities and authorizes the training abroad of teachers and prospective teachers for this purpose. Responsibility for this section of the act was delegated to the Office of Education by Presidential Executive order in 1962, with the first funds becoming available in 1964.

At the current budgetary level, approximately 1,600 individuals participate in the various OE programs abroad annually. In the present program mix, about 20 percent of these are college and university faculty members, about 35 percent are teachers or curriculum supervisors at the elementary and secondary school levels, and the remaining 45 percent are college and university students (the great majority of them at the graduate level).

Program Purposes and Priorities

The Office of Education programs, like those of all Federal agencies, are conducted in accordance with agency mission and with relevant agency guidelines and priorities. The general purpose of most OE programs in international studies, both in the U.S. and abroad, is to strengthen American education in foreign languages, area studies, and world affairs to help meet the needs of education, government, and business for skilled manpower, instructional materials, and new knowledge. Because of past neglect in the American educational system of most of the world outside Western Europe and because of funding limitations, most OE program efforts apart from Teacher Exchange have concentrated largely on the non-Western world. The Teacher Exchange program is oriented primarily toward the more economically developed nations, especially those in Western Europe. Recent IIS program initiatives in the United States at the post-secondary level include attention to Western Europe and interregional comparative studies, but dollar funds are not yet available for related activity abroad.

The OE programs abroad aim to expand and improve the capabilities of individuals as well as of institutions. As a general rule, only those activities are funded which require an overseas setting or which can be done more effectively abroad. Particularly in the preparation of specialists and in university faculty and institutional development programs concerned with the non-Western world, the opportunities provided abroad are often closely coordinated with related IIS activities in the United States under the NDEA Title VI program.

Some of the overseas programs of the Office of Education are targeted by IIS on specific objectives (for example, advanced language training in Japanese and Chinese). At the current budgetary level, in the targeted programs the IIS priorities for specialized training and research in international studies are determined primarily on the basis of critical gaps or shortages, educational capabilities which the national interest will require on a continuing basis, and anticipation of important emerging needs. Certain program efforts reflect official OE priorities such as early childhood education and education for the handicapped.

However, most OE projects abroad follow the program priorities established by American institutions for expanding and improving their specialized programs and/or strengthening the international dimensions of their general education programs. The insitution-oriented projects are normally designed by the institutions themselves and submitted at their initiative to meet their own particular needs and circumstances.

Thus, the total OE effort abroad represents a mix of activities at varying levels of specialization. For example, one OE project abroad may involve secondary school social studies supervisors while another may serve a university linguist specializing in oriental languages. The Office of Education is concerned with helping State departments of education gear up for their special leadership responsibilities in an increasingly interdependent world; assisting teacher education institutions in modernizing their curricula; and facilitating the efforts of State colleges and universities in developing new kinds of interdisciplinary graduate programs that utilize comparative, cross-cultural approaches to transnational problems or topics of common concern.

Under present funding constraints, top priority for the use of the geographically unrestricted funds available directly to OE – the Fulbright-Hays dollars – has been given to graduate students in international studies who have reached the doctoral dissertation stage in the academic pipeline. The OE fellowships enable them to complete their specialized training with appropriate field experience and thus increase the nation's stock of well qualified manpower in international studies. The other priorities for the currently available dollar funds are intensive advanced language training abroad in selected non-Western languages, ethnic heritage summer seminars, and the Foreign Curriculum Consultant program.

If the modest increase in the FY 73 budget request for the OE Fulbright-Hays program is granted by the Congress, individual faculty research fellowships for some countries where dollars are required will be resumed on a limited basis next year. A total of approximately 20 fellowships of 3- to 6-months' duration is projected for 1973-74. The program focus will be on East and Southeast Asia and on the Soviet Union and Eastern Europe. Preference will be given to research topics related to contemporary issues.

How OE Programs Differ

As will be apparent in the material that follows, in some respects the overseas programs of OE are similar to various parts of the Fulbright program which are carried out abroad under the aegis of the Department of State and in conjunction with the Board of Foreign Scholarships. However, the OE programs differ in some important respects, and they deserve appreciation on their own merits. There is very little overlap; the Department of State and Office of Education efforts complement each other nicely.

Apart from the focus on benefiting American education, the Office of Education programs differ from some others in that they de-emphasize direct, short-term political aspects. The general rationale for the OE programs emphasizes serving the national interest by strengthening the international dimensions of the American educational system, particularly through programs that help develop continuing institutional capability. In the more specialized programs, especially those with long lead times in the training of specialists — such as in Chinese studies — the long standing OE policy of continuing attention to the needs of the longer haul has clearly proven its value.

Programs may be carried out in virtually any country where they are welcome. While always alert to new program opportunities as a result of an improvement in diplomatic relations between the U.S. and another country, or of political liberalization within a host country, neither the choice of country nor of subject is particularly affected by fluctuating short-term political considerations, except in those relatively few instances where the host country reduces or suspends all relationships with the U.S. or when it may judge a project proposal to be too sensitive for current conditions. (All projects require concurrence by the host country.)

The general assumption is that sound educational programs will make their own positive contribution to foreign policy while serving educational goals. The assumption is well validated by experience.

A further difference is the sizable short-term program carried out during the summer months when teachers' schedules permit them to be available for training and curriculum development activities abroad. These programs are most commonly 5- or 8-week seminars and workshops under the sponsorship of an American college, university, or State department of education, often in cooperation with one or more school systems. Frequently several American institutions cooperate in a consortium. Most group projects abroad are normally conducted in cooperation with an educational institution in the host country. Well-planned programs of a summer's duration have repeatedly proven their value in developing some genuine understanding and appreciation for another culture and in stimulating or improving attention to related educational activities in the institutions from which the participants come.

While the main thrust in most of OE's international programs is on helping the American educational system reflect more adequately the world in which we live, the concept of mutuality is fully appreciated and has been long encouraged, particularly in Teacher Exchange. A special program, the Inter-Institutional Cooperative Research Abroad program, was initiated 2 years ago specifically to foster joint effort on priority educational problems of common concern. Many of the recent more specialized efforts in cooperative research on educational matters of common concern have been carried out under other OE legislative authority via participation in multi-lateral programs like those of the Organization for Economic Cooperation and Development (OECD).

OE is engaged in a variety of other cooperative educational endeavors for the sharing of ideas and experience through the International Bureau of Education (IBE) of UNESCO and other intergovernmental organizations like the Organization of American States (OAS). In a related activity, IIS helps recruit American educators for service in the field programs of UNESCO. Other important program efforts have been carried out on a bilateral basis by such OE units as the National Center for Educational Research and Development and the National Center for Educational Communication. Most international activities concerned with basic pedagogical research and information systems will henceforth be the responsibility of the new HEW agency for educational research, the National Institute of Education, rather than of the Office of Education.

Project Planning and Selection of Participants

While deadlines differ for the various IIS grant and contract programs, October 1 is the most common annual deadline for submitting proposals for projects to be implemented the following summer or academic year. The initiative for project planning rests mainly with the educational community. All proposals are carefully evaluated by educational consultants or field readers and by staff specialists. All Fulbright-Hays proposals are further reviewed by both the Board of Foreign Scholarships and American Embassy and host government officials in the countries concerned. All Fulbright-Hays individual grantees and directors of group projects must be approved by the Board of Foreign Scholarships.

Program Categories and Examples of Projects

While OE programs abroad serve various purposes, there are some kinds of activities that do not fall within OE priorities. For example, the Institute does not support student exchange programs, or regular junior-year-abroad programs, or general educational tours for teachers or students, or programs of financial assistance to foreign students. Valuable as such activities are, they fall outside the present OE program priorities and funding limitations but within the missions and objectives of other public agencies and nongovernmental organizations.[1]

In the OE programs carried out abroad, OE objectives are served through exchange teaching, research, training, and curriculum development activities. At the present budget level there is a special interest in instructional personnel, materials preparation, and curriculum development because of the multiplier effect inherent in them. The various kinds of activities in which virtually all participants abroad are engaged may be summarized in the following categories.

Exchange Teaching

The OE Institute of International Studies cooperates with the Bureau of Educational and Cultural Affairs in the Department of State in administering the Teacher Exchange Program authorized by the Fulbright-Hays Act. The exchange of teachers may involve direct interchanges — school for school, grade for grade, and subject for subject — or the one-way placement of American elementary and secondary school teachers abroad and teachers from other countries in American schools.

Generally speaking, interchanges are carried out with the nations of Western Europe or with English-speaking countries elsewhere. The interchange of elementary teachers occurs only with the English-speaking countries. American teachers on one-way assignments abroad most often teach English as a foreign language or American civilization courses. Teachers from other countries in the United States on a one-way basis normally teach languages such as Spanish, French, German, Latin, and sometimes Japanese, Swedish, and Finnish. Some teachers have taught mathematics, history, or the sciences.

About 135 American teachers will be teaching in 13 countries in 1972-73. Conversely, about 135 teachers from 15 countries will teach in elementary and secondary schools and in some community colleges in the United States, making a total of about 270 teachers and 23 different countries involved. Americans abroad on interchange assignments will number about 100 in five countries. Thirty American teachers will be on one-way assignments in 10 countries. Conversely, approximately 100 teachers from five countries will be placed in American schools on an interchange basis and about 35 teachers from 11 countries on a one-way basis.

---

[1] For a comprehensive review of other Federal programs, both in the U.S. and abroad, see *Inventory of Federal Programs Involving Educational Activities Concerned with Improving International Understanding and Cooperation*, 545 pages, published by IIS in 1969 and available from the Superintendent of Documents, U.S. Government Printing Office, at $4.75 per copy. The Inventory summarizes 159 programs from 31 different agencies. While outdated now in some respects, this volume remains the most comprehensive and useful reference work on Federal activities in international education.

Individual Research

Doctoral dissertation research gives opportunities for advanced graduate students to engage in full-time dissertation research abroad for 6 to 12 months in modern foreign languages, area studies, and world affairs. This program is designed to help develop research knowledge and capability in world areas not widely included in American curricula, and help prospective teachers and scholars enhance their knowledge of a foreign country or region, its peoples, and its languages.

Faculty research fellowships are opportunities for specialists in international studies to engage in full-time research and study abroad for 6 to 12 months in modern foreign languages, area studies, and world affairs. This program is designed to help keep key faculty members current in their specialties, extend the range of competence of established scholars, produce new knowledge through research, and assist institutions in updating curricula and in improving instructional materials.

Linguistic studies and preparation of instructional materials on foreign language, area studies, and world affairs – in conjunction with Section 602 of Title VI of the National Defense Education Act – includes such undertakings as a contrastive analysis of the sound systems, grammars, and lexicons of Serbo-Croatian and English. It also includes the preparation of Polish language teaching materials and the preparation of a handbook of research resources on East Central and Southeastern Europe that are located in those regions. (Estimated 1972-73 size of program: seven projects.)

Comparative education studies include country studies, preparation of bibliographies, and translation of selected foreign publications on education. These represent a small but important group of activities in support of the Office of Education's continuing responsibility for keeping abreast of educational developments in other countries.

Inter-institutional cooperative research covers comparative and cross-cultural studies of 1 to 2 years' duration carried out jointly by American educational institutions or State departments of education with institutions abroad on educational problems, processes, and procedures which the cooperating countries share in common and which reflect Office of Education priorities for research needed in improving American education. Examples of subjects include early childhood education, education for the handicapped, and comparative studies on urban and environmental problems. Projects in this category are normally joint projects of IIS and other OE bureaus.

Advanced Language Training

Advanced training in special year-long intensive programs has been projected in critical non-Western languages such as Japanese, Chinese, Arabic, and Hindi-Urdu. The Office of Education helps support the American interuniversity programs in Tokyo, Taipei, and Cairo which provide the most advanced training regularly available abroad to American students of Japanese, Chinese, and Arabic. The program in Tokyo is cosponsored with the Japanese Government and the Ford Foundation; the one in Taipei with the Ford Foundation. Advanced training in special intensive summer programs in Russian, and in other important languages for which suitable instruction is available in excess foreign currency countries (including such languages as Polish, Serbo-Croatian, Arabic and Hindi-Urdu), are also projected.

Ethnic Heritage Seminars

Summer seminars and workshops related to domestic ethnic heritage programs which focus on the cultural origins of minority groups in the United States and on the development of intercultural understanding in American education are planned. The projects are sponsored by State departments of education or colleges and universities in cooperation with school systems. The participants are primarily elementary and secondary school teachers and curriculum supervisors engaged in conducting or planning ethnic studies programs. Areas and countries emphasized in 1972-73 were West Africa, Japan, China, Mexico, Poland, and Yugoslavia.

Other Group Training and Curriculum Development Projects

Projects normally of 2- to 12-months' duration are aimed at training, curriculum development, and/or preparation or acquisition of instructional materials for programs in international and intercultural studies. The projects are sponsored by U.S. educational insitutions or non-profit educational organizations.

The principal criteria used in evaluating proposals for Group Projects Abroad include: (1) The project's relevance to the institution's or organization's educational goals and its relationship to the applicant's program development plans in foreign languages, area studies, and world affairs; (2) The feasibility of the project and the capability of the applicant to carry it out; (3) The extent to which direct experience abroad is necessary to achieve the project's objectives and the effectiveness with which relevant host country resources would be utilized; (4) Program priorities as determined by the Office of Education. Preference will be given to projects concerning foreign languages and geographic areas which are of continuing concern to the national interest and for which adequate instruction has not been widely available in the United States. (5) The potential impact of the project on the development of foreign language, area studies, and world affairs programs in American education.

Participants may include college and university faculty members, deans of instruction and coordinators of world affairs programs in community colleges, educational leaders at the State level, curriculum consultants and supervisors, school administrators with responsibility for leadership in educational innovation, experienced elementary and secondary school teachers, and selected graduate and advanced undergraduate students specializing in foreign language and area studies. Increasing priority is being given to programs which assist State departments of education, teacher education programs, large school systems, developing institutions, and groups of community colleges. Some examples of representative projects from recent years would include:

- An intensive summer seminar on urban studies in Yugoslavia, for 18 faculty members and six advanced students engaged in the improvement of comparative studies in the 12 institutions in threé States that make up the Great Lakes Colleges Association.

- An intensive summer program on Serbo-Croatian language and Yugoslav area studies including formal study at the Zagreb Institute, home stays, and a correlated field trip to rural areas, for 21 graduate and advanced undergraduate students of Eastern European studies from Portland State University and other American institutions.

- An 11-week program of lectures, seminars, and field work in Yugoslavia for 22 American students of geography who were preparing to specialize in Eastern Europe.

- An experimental 1-month field seminar to introduce the chief State school officers of eight American States and six members of State boards of education to the non-Western world. The firsthand exposure to Japan, India, and Israel enabled them to make a preliminary assessment of the adequacy with which these important nations were reflected in the curricula of the schools in their States, and make plans for needed improvement. They were also able to study selected aspects of the educational systems of those countries and establish professional contacts with their counterparts. The program began with an introduction to Asia conducted at the East-West Center in Hawaii.

- Members of the Tennessee State Department of Education traveled to Tunisia and parts of East Africa to develop instructional materials on contemporary Africa for use throughout the school systems of Tennessee.

- An 8-week seminar and materials preparation program in India for 20 social science supervisors and curriculum directors from 16 states.

- An interracial group of 30 public school teachers from southern Georgia studied in India for a summer in preparation for introducing Indian studies into the Georgia school curriculum on multicultural understanding.

- Twenty-one curriculum specialists and teachers from Shippensburg State College, Hagerstown Junior College, and the Washington County Schools in Maryland planned and prepared curricula and instructional materials in India for use in their home institutions. Results include development of a graduate level course in curriculum development, a course in Indian culture for elementary and secondary teachers unable to participate in the field seminar, and compilation of materials for a series on comparative religions and world cultures to be presented on the closed circuit television system linking all 45 of the Washington County Schools.

Some Plans for the Year Ahead

Center for Arabic Studies Abroad

Twenty full-year graduate students and 30 summer students, each with at least 2 years' previous study of Arabic, will engage in a formal program of intensive language and area study at the American University in Cairo. The program is conducted by the Center for Arabic Studies Abroad (CASA), a consortium of nine American universities created to improve American teaching and scholarship related to the Middle East. Students are recruited through national competitions. The instructional materials developed at CASA are made available to institutions in the United States.

American Institute of Indian Studies

Fifteen American graduate students in South Asian studies, selected through a national competition by the American Institute of Indian Studies, will participate in a 9-month program of intensive advanced instruction at an Indian university in one of three major Indian languages: Hindi-Urdu, Marathi, or Tamil.

Alliance College (Pennsylvania)

Thirteen graduate students and one faculty director from Alliance College will spend an academic year at Jagellonian University in Krakow, Poland, to study the Polish language and culture. The program is designed to promote Polish studies in the United States by increasing the number of highly trained Polish language specialists. More than half of the students at Alliance College are of Polish descent and the school is the only accredited U.S. college with a fully developed curriculum in Polish studies.

Fairmont State College (West Virginia)

Twenty college faculty members in the humanities, arts, social sciences or education, principally from the 31 member institutions of the Regional Council on International Education, are scheduled to participate in an 8-week summer program at the American University in Cairo. Participants will prepare teaching materials in order to develop or augment undergraduate courses on comtemporary Egypt.

Seton Hall University (New Jersey)

A faculty research team from Seton Hall University will engage in research projects in Poland and gather materials to form the basis for courses in comparative management, international marketing, and a history of modern Poland. The five participants represent the fields of history, international studies, business, economics, and finance. After appropriate evaluation, the materials will be incorporated in the curriculum of Seton Hall's Institute of International Business and in a new Polish area studies program, and thus enable Seton Hall to better serve the more than 1 million Americans of Polish or Eastern European descent living in New Jersey.·

Temple University (Pennsylvania)

Twenty-five high school teachers from Bucks County, Pa., and faculty members from Temple University are scheduled to participate in a summer curriculum development project in Morocco. The project will improve the ability of Bucks County teachers to meet recent State requirements for interdisciplinary courses in world culture and will help Temple University, a major producer of educational manpower in southeast Pennsylvania, upgrade offerings on non-Western cultures. Participants will design kits for teaching about North Africa in Bucks County schools and in the 60 colleges and universities which comprise the Pennsylvania Council for International Education.

New York University

An innovative master of arts program at New York University which prepares students to teach non-Western studies in secondary schools will be enriched by a curriculum development seminar in India. Twenty-five teachers and prospective teachers of Asian studies are scheduled to spend a summer studying under Indian professors and developing curriculum materials for use in American schools and colleges. The summer program in India is part of the graduate offerings in Comparative Cultures at New York University and is the first phase of a 3-summer program leading to an M.A. in the teaching of Asian Studies.

An Important Beginning

In facing the realities of today's interdependent world, American education has begun to come to grips with three crucial facts:

- The intellectual boundary lines between problems commonly labeled "foreign" and "domestic" are often artificial and misleading.

- A general education at any school level is incomplete without an international dimension.

- It is essential for every citizen to understand more about the ethnic diversity and cultural pluralism of our times.

The task of reducing ethnocentrism at all levels of American education is a vast undertaking. For example, there are approximately 2,500,000 teachers and administrators in the elementary and secondary schools of the United States and more than 2,500 colleges and universities. The overwhelming majority of American teachers at all levels have had no professional preparation in international studies and no experience abroad with other cultures, particularly with respect to the non-Western world.

While the funds available from all sources in the public and private sectors combined are small in relation to the total task, the Office of Education is endeavoring to make its contribution to international understanding through available resources. Each year the various OE programs described here are helping to accelerate the achievement of a deeper understanding of mankind around the globe and the development of more relevance in American education through opportunities for teaching, research, training, and curriculum development abroad.

Such first hand experience in other countries is essential for a number of present and prospective scholars, teachers, and other key educational leaders if American schools, colleges, and universities are going to be able to deal effectively with the educational implications of an increasingly interdependent world. Of special significance is the continuing contribution that educational programs can make to improving the level of citizen literacy in world affairs. Thus in a variety of ways the Office of Education programs abroad help underpin President Nixon's imaginative initiatives toward a generation of peace.

Chapter 5

UNESCO AND AMERICAN EDUCATION

John E. Fobes and Paul Coste

American Education Abroad is an effort to take stock of the many interfaces between education in the United States in 1973 and other educational systems around the world. In this chapter, we examine some of the ways in which U.S. education is related to the world-wide work of the United Nations Educational, Scientific and Cultural Organization (UNESCO). We are concerned about the impact of American educational thought and the ways it can contribute to education abroad. We are also interested in the impact of other cultures on American education and how American education can be enriched through its association with UNESCO. Looking ahead we can anticipate some of UNESCO's requirements for ideas, techniques and personnel. The reader may be able to sense how UNESCO, an organization serving all of its Member States, looks out on a world in which education everywhere is in a state of ferment.

Since 1946, UNESCO has been the principal instrument by which its Member States, now numbering 130, share some of their concerns for education. At first, UNESCO served as a clearing house for information and a forum where the members could work together on measures to promote human rights and the development of education in all countries. In the last fifteen years, the UNESCO program has become steadily more active in mobilizing aid for education in what we have called the developing countries. As more and more resources have become available, especially through the United Nations Development Program and the International Bank for Reconstruction and Development, the program has become more deeply involved in operational assistance to Member States in the resolution of specific problems, such as training teachers, organizing universities and creating new curricula. UNESCO has become a major force for the renovation of education and the extension of educational opportunity to all parts of the population. In recent years, in fact, the UNESCO Secretariat has become a friendly counsellor to member countries at all stages of development.[1]

It is against this evolving background that we will examine some issues which may be of interest to those who are engaged in the guidance or preparation of professional educators in America. We shall first review the likely future thrust of the UNESCO activity in education. To what extent is it likely to grow? What demands will this growth make on the world reservoir of educational expertise? How does UNESCO go about providing advice to countries on their educational policies and plans and relating them to manpower and other needs in each country's plan for economic and social

[1] See *Learning to Be*, Report of the International Commission on Educational Development, Unesco — Paris 1972. Harrap, London

development? Finally, we will examine the implications for American educators of UNESCO's role as an international centre for communications in education.

From the present UNESCO program, one can see three main themes or groups of activities which will carry on into the next six years? UNESCO will promote the expansion of systems of education to provide access to basic education for all children, and to support economic and social development. Secondly, UNESCO will strive to improve the quality of educational systems, especially in the developing countries, by helping with the renewal of the structures, curricula and methods of education and of teacher training. Thirdly, UNESCO will seek to enlarge the scope of education so that it can be more responsive to societal needs and the great human problems of our time.

These goals have been translated into a number of objectives which reveal the nature of research which will be promoted, the types of symposia and seminars organized, the topics which will be the subject of publications, the kind of training courses which will be sponsored and the type of expert assistance which will be needed:

1. Assisting countries to formulate educational policies which promote easier access to education in all its forms, and which support social and economic development.

2. Helping to elaborate plans for educational development which harmonize with economic development. This means building close relations between study and the world of work.

3. Promoting new structures of education which provide greater flexibility to meet the needs and aspirations of the students. This means development of the concept of life-long learning, unrelated to age or socio-economic status.

4. Renewing the curricula and assuring the balance between general, scientific and technical education. Important aspects of this renewal are the close connections between learning, the world of work and ethical pre-occupations.

5. Promotion of new methods and techniques of education which are particularly suited to each country or region.

6. Promotion of more effective preparation of teachers and educational personnel of all kinds. UNESCO's most essential role is in training teacher educators.

[2] See Unesco documents *Draft Medium-Term Outline Plan for 1973-1978* (17 C/4) and *Approved Programme and Budget for 1973-1974* (17 C/5)

7. Helping Member States to reduce the percentage of world illiteracy to 27 per cent in 1980.

8. Promoting the provision of effective adult education. This goal is especially important because of the enormous numbers of men and women, previously denied access to education, who seek self-fulfillment, culturally and professionally.

9. To ensure that education in its Member States contributes effectively to the knowledge and application of the Rights of Man, international understanding and peace.

10. To organize the educational activities of UNESCO so that the needs and aspirations of youth shall be served. This will include attention to the great issues of over-population and improvement of the quality of life.

11. UNESCO will analyze the major trends in the development of societies, so that future educational needs may be anticipated and plans concerted to meet them.

To organize and administer the catalytic work of UNESCO and to help the international community toward these objectives, the Education sector of the Secretariat is staffed with 300 professionals, located in Paris headquarters and four regional offices and coming from 60 countries. At work on projects in 85 countries are around 700 experts and associate experts, recruited from all over the world. Some serve as single advisers; most are in teams with teacher training colleges, experimental projects (for example, rural education) and institutions for educational research and planning. There is a trend toward the use of senior consultants for short periods (and repeated visits).

The pace of these activities has steadily increased in recent years. In teacher training, in curriculum reform, in all aspects of technical education, UNESCO projects, usually funded by the United Nations Development Programme or the International Bank for Reconstruction and Development, have been multiplying rapidly. The demand for qualified experts to staff those technical assistance activities has naturally increased as well. Recruitment of appropriate people seems to be a critical bottleneck in the whole process, one that is particularly complex for an international organization. For example, any government which receives technical assistance, has the right to approve or disapprove experts who are nominated to serve by UNESCO or any other international agency. The language skills of an expert must be compatible with at least the second language of the country in which he will serve. On the side of availability, the more outstanding the expert, the more difficult it is to free him from his national obligations to institution, to colleagues and to his career. Moreover, the basic procedure for recruiting is long, and usually involves lengthy periods of writing for approvals and organizing the team on which the specialist is to serve. Another problem is the temporary status of experts, who work on a fixed-term contractual basis, usually for one or two years at a time. Thus recruitment delays and the growing demand for expert services have made it more difficult for UNESCO to execute programs of assistance. The availability of competent staff has become a critical issue.

We cannot overstate the importance of certain human qualities in experts, quite apart from their professional competence. It has proved difficult indeed to predict how a person will react within a new cultural setting and with a multi-national group of colleagues. This is an area which has long called for a research effort to help us to recognize those qualities which seem to lead to success and those which handicap an expert in the performance of his duty in a foreign setting. In general we have had to rely on the experience and judgement of a few persons who seem to have a capacity for evaluating candidates in this regard.

With these factors in mind, in theory the United States should offer potentially one of the largest national sources of expertise on which international agencies can draw. The size of the US educational establishment, the allocation of resources to schools and research, the number of teacher-training institutions, the production of highly trained personnel in education, are all indicators of the great numbers who are theoretically available. Moreover, the multi-national origins of the American population should constitute a positive factor for international work. Until now, however, the USA has not been the major supplier of expertise in education, especially to UNESCO and other United Nations agencies, which one might have expected.

Are there not implications for American education at home which stem from the rising tide of assistance and cooperative investigation which is sponsored by UNESCO? The movement of several hundreds of Americans per year to assignments overseas must open new vistas. To uproot one's family, to come to grips with very different life-styles and professional behaviors has usually enlarged the perspectives of those who take part. To test one's problem-solving skills, to adapt one's knowledge to a different scene are experiences which evoke a maximum effort. Moreover, in the realm of research and investigation of learning problems, the wide variations among schools and social settings provide opportunities for cross-cultural comparisons, which may provide insights on some problem areas in American schools. For instance, building language skills, studying the effects of different child-rearing practices, and designing teaching strategies to reach children and parents whose levels of aspiration are low. Thus we can see that as technical assistance increases abroad, there will be great opportunities for professional growth in those who take part.

Some have suggested that the moment is at hand when a systematic review of the long-term needs for expert services of different categories must be undertaken together with an inventory of potential sources of experts. This would be a rather sophisticated planning exercise. It is unlikely that the existing system of recruitment will be capable of meeting the expanding needs of the next decade or two. In fact what may be needed is a basic re-examination of the nature of technical assistance projects and other cooperative devices in the field of education.

Another implication which follows the expansion of UNESCO's programs is the expectation that links between institutions in different countries will increase. The typical assistance, research or experimental project seems to run from five to ten years, and makes use of a number of international experts. The replacement of experts every two or three years creates discontinuities which may be unavoidable but often jeopardize the efficiency of projects. The changing of nationalities, professional backgrounds, and personal characteristics, as experts come and go, undermines the sense of consistency and direction of a project. In the future, we may see one component of a project, say the preparation of mathematics teachers or the evaluation of a new methodology, assigned to an institution which will be asked to staff a post continuously over the whole life of a project, with a succession of experts from that institution and to provide certain services at its headquarters. The successive incumbents of a specialist post in the other country would share a point of view and would know their predecessors. Moreover, counterpart nationals could be trained in the cooperating institution where a familiarity with the problems of the developing country would make the training more effective.

When considering such an institutional link, we should be careful to preserve the international character of UNESCO technical assistance. A project employing four experts should have perhaps four contracts with institutions in different countries to preserve the multi-national aspect while ensuring greater continuity. Moreover, it would be possible under this pattern to use a sort of differenciated staffing. A full professor might be in charge of planning and initiating project activities. An assistant professor might carry on while the professor returned to his institution for several months. Graduate students and even undergraduates might make important contributions on a volunteer basis, while carrying out work related to their degree programs. The professor, on subsequent, short-term visits, could evaluate progress, recommend changes, etc. In short, the university could be fully engaged on several levels to ensure the success of its component, at no greater cost than that of a single isolated expert as now deployed. Both the institution and the developing country would derive real advantages from this new concept.

An appropriate caution here is that the contracting institution should accept such work not only because it feels an obligation owed to the developing world but also because it sees mutual benefits. The advantages in these arrangements for an institution in training its own staff and students, in research opportunities, and in international goodwill can be significant. To make these arrangements acceptable, of course, they must be seen by the assisted country to provide clearly more and better service than the existing system of deploying individual experts.

The Communications Role

Since the founding of UNESCO in 1946, one of the general objectives of the Organization has been to promote the flow of information between Member States. In education, this objective has been served by a broad program of publications, through documentation services, through the collection and dissemination of statistics on education, and through hundreds of meetings on all kinds of educational problems. Ranging from the large-scale Regional Conferences of Ministers of Education, down to small study groups of five to ten experts, these UNESCO meetings have brought together scholars and policy-makers from all over the world to focus on the problems of education. Participating countries have been helped to focus on important problems, to generate new approaches to common problems, to identify sources of international assistance. Moreover, these meetings have brought together men and women who might otherwise never have met. They have developed informal communications links which partially overcome the isolation they often feel in their jobs. An international community of educators is coming into existence which provides intangible but real support for the improvement of education everywhere. The decentralization of many UNESCO activities from the Secretariat to its four regional offices will help to increase communication among educators. These centres will provide documentation and resident experts in a number of fields which are closer to the users than the Secretariat in Paris.

The future UNESCO program will, if anything, intensify the links between educators. The International Bureau of Education at Geneva has embarked on building a computerized data bank for educational documentation and research, not unlike the American ERIC system. Abstracts from many countries are already being disseminated to the UNESCO Member States, and linkages with three or four existing information systems are planned.

Apart from these practical services, it may be noted here that UNESCO is generally becoming communications-oriented, placing increaisng emphasis in its work on the technical means of disseminating information and instruction. The Secretariat is providing advice on regional communications satellites and on tele-education in general. Radio transmission in some areas offers the best means of reaching children and adults with enriched learning programs. Instructional materials in many languages must be foreseen as well as ways to evaluate such innovative activities.

One conclusion from this trend towards increasing the communication role of the Organization is that more expert services in radio, television, programmed instruction, curriculum building, evaluative research, etc., will be required.

Americans in the field of education would do well to inform themselves more about UNESCO. They are going to be asked to contribute more in the future in the way of expert services and information. Moreover, as the purposes and place of education in societies all over the world are transformed and techniques modified, America can learn from others and from cooperating with them. What better framework for this mutual learning and supportive process than UNESCO, an organization in the founding of which America played a principal role!

Chapter 6

DEVELOPMENT OF THE COMMUNITY COLLEGE CONCEPT ABROAD

Raymond E. Schultz

INTRODUCTION

For the reader who is unfamiliar with the phrase "community college concept" as used in the United States, it refers to the multiple purposes served by most of our public junior colleges and in part by our two-year private colleges. These purposes are represented by programs which prepare students for direct employment, programs which prepare students for upper-division college and university study, and programs for adults which range from employment retraining and upgrading to study for personal interest. Frequently student services such as guidance, counseling, and special assistance for students with educational deficiencies are listed as functions of a community college. However, since the focus of this treatment is on educational programs and institutional structure, those services are not discussed. This report focuses on the extent to which such programs offered in institutions outside of the United States are similar to our community junior colleges.

BACKGROUND

A series of related conditions occuring particularly in developing countries is having important implications for the educational purposes served by American community junior colleges.

One of these conditions is the growing number of secondary school graduates for whom there is inadequate opportunity for further educational training. This is the result of the recently expanded systems of elementary and secondary education in these countries. While most of these nations have not achieved anything approaching mass secondary education, or even mass elementary education, the output of secondary school graduates is increasing rapidly and will continue to do so.

A second condition is a growing number of university graduates for whom there are no employment opportunities related to their university studies. Partly this is the result of the expansion of traditional university programs, often with foreign assistance. Partly it is the result of the long standing tradition in these countries that university graduation, in whatever curriculum, means "desk work" as contrasted to "physical work."

57

A third condition is a shortage of personnel who possess specialized skills in technical, semi-professional, and mid-management fields. This is a result of several related factors. One is a lack of programs in these fields, due in part at least to the fact that until relatively recently there were few demands for such workers. Another is that the overriding purpose of secondary education has been to prepare students for traditional university studies.

These three conditions are increasingly confronting governmental officials of developing countries with serious problems and dilemas. The growing number of secondary school graduates for whom there is no place in the universities is beginning to have political repercussions of major proportions. For example, in Venezuela in 1972, it was estimated by educational officials that there were over 70,000 secondary school graduates who had passed the stiff university entrance examinations but for whom there was no place in the universities. Collins cites similar figures for Ceylon.[1] The response in Thailand to the political pressure created by the growing number of secondary school graduates was the establishment in 1970 of an "open university" to which all youth who had passed the university entrance examinations were assured admission. Of the over 40,000 students enrolled in this institution (Ramkhamhaeng University), more than 8,000 of them are reportedly studying law. This hardly relates to Thailand's manpower needs nor does it constitute prudent use of that country's limited economic resources.

Many countries may be creating an even more dangerous political monster than the one presented by the growing number of secondary school graduates if they take the road being traveled by Thailand. Graduating several thousand additional lawyers a year, for whom there are few appropriate employment opportunities, poses ominous political consequences to say nothing of the implications that such an imbalance has for relating educational policies to national priorities.

These conditions suggest that the time is ripe for many countries, especially developing ones, to give more attention to community college type education. However, as is always the case with social institutions, there are traditions, vested interests, and a host of practical considerations which work against such a development.

The educational systems of most developing countries, whether Africa, Asia, or South America, were patterned after those of European countries which colonized them or otherwise had a major influence on their development. Consequently a number of changes are needed before the American version of the community junior college can be successfully introduced. One of these is the virtual autonomy of each faculty, i.e. school

---

[1] Charles C. Collins, "Exporting the Junior College Idea," *International Development of the Junior College Idea*. American Association of Junior Colleges, Washington, D.C. 1970, pp. 156-68.

or college, within a university. Another, closely related to the previous one, is the virtual impossibility of student transfer from one institution to another or even from one program to another within a university. Also, in many of these universities the credit unit system does not exist. A student's success in a course is determined almost exclusively by an end-of-the-year examination. In some countries, however, there is a gradual shift to credit units and semester calendars rather than year-long courses.

Another factor which mitigates against the introduction of the American comprehensive community college model is that the mainstream of secondary education is geared exclusively to the preparation of students for traditional university academic studies. At several points during the elementary and secondary school period, there are externally administered examinations which either terminate or divert into vocational programs students who "fail" these exams. "Fail" in this context means all of those who do not pass the matriculation examinations, regardless of how close they come to doing so or the extent to which they may excel in certain areas. As if that were not enough pressure on secondary school students, many of those who pass the university entrance examinations are not admitted because of strict enrollment quotas. It is no wonder then that great importance is placed on gaining entrance into traditional universities and that many youth who fail to do so have little interest in or background for occupational programs below the university level. Because of this "creaming" process, most parents who have the financial means send their children to private elementary and secondary schools to increase the probability that they will be able to pass the university entrance examinations. Further, families with the most means send their children to the most expensive and the best of these private schools.

Another change that would need to be made before an institution like our comprehensive community junior college could succeed is societal recognition of the graduates. At present the major employer of university graduates in these countries is the government. With a surplus of such graduates there seems little likelihood that employment requirements for government positions which pay a livable salary will be altered regardless of the specialized competencies and talents possessed by applicants who do not possess university degrees. This does not preclude the employment of such individuals in business and industry.

There is also the need to understand this component of education and how it might logically be part of an overall educational system. Strong leadership will be required to make significant changes in the existing educational structures of these countries. This requirement is an especially difficult one to meet. Ministers of education in developing countries come and go like the seasons. Even where one may remain in the position for a reasonable length of time, he is likely to be a medical doctor, lawyer, or engineer with no previous experience in the field of education. While the supporting staffs of these ministries generally enjoy longer tenure, few of them have an understanding of our community college concept. Added to that difficulty is the fact in most countries that the ministry of education has only limited involvement in policies relating to university education. Since university rectors likewise tend to have short tenure, each faculty within a university pretty much runs its own show. Understandably they display little interest in short-cycle, higher education.

Finally, there are limitations of resources – both financial and human. The expansion of elementary and secondary education has placed a severe financial strain on many developing countries. This situation is further aggrevated by the fact that many of them are also putting greatly increased funds into their universities. It is understandable then that the educational policy makers of these countries are reluctant to expand post-secondary education. Part of this reluctance is due to the fact that education in these countries has never been viewed in terms of human needs and economic return.

This combination of factors suggests a pessimistic future so far as the establishment of comprehensive community college type institutions overseas is concerned. But there is another side to the coin. The winds of change are blowing – and strongly in some instances. As noted previously, the pressures of numbers alone is bringing political and educational policy makers to a realization that the traditional educational structures and programs are not adequate. There are also indications that policy makers are beginning to give serious attention to human needs and potential economic returns when establishing educational priorities. The forms that these efforts are taking vary, depending upon educational traditions and leadership. To illustrate, a brief review of developments in selected countries follows.

AN OVERVIEW OF DEVELOPMENTS IN SELECTED COUNTRIES

Developments in Asia

JAPAN. The most extensive junior college development in Asia is found in Japan. This type of institution was introduced there in 1949 on the recommendation of Walter C. Eels, while he was serving as educational advisor to General McArthur. Japan now has nearly 500 of these institutions, the majority of which are private schools for young women. Many of them offer only general studies in the humanities and homemaking. However, most of Japan's kindergarten teachers are prepared in these institutions and business education programs are growing. There are approximately seventy-five junior colleges for young men which offer programs in such areas as agriculture and industrial technology.

These junior colleges do not offer transfer programs. The fact that most of them are private — as are most university enrollments in Japan — means that they serve a selected economic group. Even so they are experiencing financial difficulty. A major effort is being made to obtain financial support for them from the government.

SOUTH KOREA. Fourteen junior colleges were established in the Republic of Korea following the Korean war. They have not had a successful history. Here seems to be a classic case of attempting to transplant an American educational institution into another country without making needed adjustments and without an understanding of the concept or a commitment to it by educational leaders of the country.

A number of two- and three-year technical junior colleges and junior teachers colleges have also been established in Korea. Some of these are operated as private institutions, in some cases private universities, and some are public institutions. The Korean Ministry of Education recognizes the merit of community college type programs. However, officials there are uncertain as to what steps should be taken to enable these institutions to realize their potential.

SOUTH VIETNAM. The Vietnamese educational system was patterned after the French system — without the modification which France's system has undergone during the past twenty years. This means that it is elitist and in large measure unrelated to the country's manpower needs. Each university faculty is largely autonomous. Instruction is casual, with professors selling their lecture notes which students attempt to memorize in order to pass the end-of-course examinations. The Faculty of Law, at the University of Saigon, with an enrollment of 14,000 students, has as its facilities a former kindergarten school. This disregard for the importance of environment reflects the difference between their concept and the American concept of higher education.

There is, however, a growing awareness on the part of educational leaders of the shortcomings of their present system and measures are being taken to change it. One is a recent decision to develop a system of community colleges. Sites have been selected for the first two of these institutions and planning is underway to build facilities, select the staff, and develop programs.[2] The future of this effort will depend in part upon the military and political developments of that war-torn country. Nevertheless, there are competent persons in the Ministry of Education who understand the community college concept and who are committed to it. In addition, a

[2] Khe Ba Do, "The Community College in Vietnam," *Junior College Journal*, 42: 16-19, November 1971.

number of Vietnamese graduate students in the United States are specializing in community college administration. It appears that South Vietnam will not repeat the mistakes which were made when the junior college was introduced in the Republic of Korea.

THAILAND. Higher education in Thailand has undergone major expansion in recent years. Several new universities have opened, as have a number of two- and three-year technical and teachers colleges operated by the Ministry of Education. Some of these teachers colleges have been converted to universities and there is pressure to convert others. Only public institutions are authorized to award university degrees in Thailand.

As has been noted, even with this expansion, Thailand has not been able to meet the demand for higher education. Conequently, and largely as a politically expedient measure, Ramkhamhaeng University was opened in 1970. It is an "open door" institution for all youth who have passed the university entrance examination. Enrollment has ballooned to about 40,000. Unfortunately, its programs bear little relationship to Thailand's manpower needs. This means that it represents a major drain on Thailand's financial resources without the promise of a future corresponding contribution to the country's economy and human services needs.

Efforts have been made to expand short-cycle higher education in Thailand. Seven technical colleges have many more applicants than can be accommodated with existing faculties and staffs. One result of this is the establishment of numerous private institutes. They are expensive, unsupervised, and, in many cases, of questionable quality.

The Ministry of Education has considered establishing junior colleges, though it seems unlikely that such action will be taken. Serious discussion is underway, however, at Chulalongkorn University (the most prestigious university in Thailand) relative to their establishing a junior college in Chalburi, a city about 50 miles from Bangkok. A site has been obtained for that purpose and a planning committee at Chulalongkorn is seriously considering the matter.

SINGAPORE. Singapore represents an unusual setting because of its small area, high level of economic development, homogenous population (about 85 percent of Chinese origin), and its long period of British rule. Hong Kong is similar to Singapore in many respects, but, of course, it is still a British possesion. Each system operates both English and Chinese language schools through the university level.

Singapore's educational system has retained strong British characteristics. Many of the administrators and faculty have studied in Britain. In 1970 there was opened in Singapore an institution named The National Junior College. However, the name is misleading in terms of American usage. It actually represents the sixth form of the British educational system which is roughly equivalent to grades 12 and 13 of our academic programs. National Junior College "creams" the students who complete the fifth form of education and gives them a highly academic university preparatory program. This institution has been very successful in terms of the purpose for which it was created. Plans are underway to build more such junior colleges.

Paralleling these university preparatory junior colleges are two technical programs including some for fifth form students (grades 8-10). These programs are designed to prepare graduates for employment and have considerable appeal to young people. There are many more applicants for admission to these technical colleges than can be accomodated. A proposal is under consideration to open a polytechnic university (degree granting technological university). If this is done, graduates of the technical colleges who pass external examinations would be eligible to transfer to this new university.

AFGHANISTAN. At present post-secondary education in Afghanistan is largely limited to Kabul University with an enrollment of about 4,000, although there are several two-year teacher training institutions and a number of special institutes with small enrollments operated by the various ministries of the government.

A committee known as the National Committee on Junior Colleges has been appointed to advise the Minister of Education on the establishment of junior colleges. A member of that committee has prepared a plan for the development of community junior colleges in Afghanistan.[3] There are five cities other than Kabul which have populations of 50,000 and over. The plan proposes that a community junior college be established in each of these cities to offer both transfer and occupational programs. Since financing education in Afghanistan is extremely difficult, the existing teacher training institutions could be converted into comprehensive junior colleges. The Committee is of the opinion that the establishment of junior colleges in cities outside of Kabul would both promote the development of those cities and reduce the migration of young people to Kabul.

Developments in South America

VENEZUELA. Major developments are taking place in Venezuelan higher education. These began several years ago with the establishment of two new universities by the Ministry of Education; Oriente in the eastern part of the country, and Simon Bolivar on the outskirts of Caracas. Also established in recent years were a high level technological university with United Nations

---

[3] Abdul Ali Kandari, *A Junior College System for Afghanistan*, Faculty of Education, University of Kabul, Kabul, Afghanistan, 1970.

support and a French-type technical institute with assistance from the French government.

Even with these encouraging activities, there is a rapid increase in the number of secondary school graduates who have qualified for university entrance but cannot be admitted. Reference to this situation was made previously. In part, this is because Central University in Caracas, an autonomous public institution with a normal enrollment of 30,000, has been closed most of the time in recent years by student strikes.

Plans are now underway to establish a number of junior colleges offering both transfer and occupational programs. The first two were scheduled to open late in 1972. Concurrently, plans are underway to open Simon Rodriquez University, an upper-division university which will receive its students from these junior colleges. This is a development that warrants watching. If successful, it could set a pattern for other countries that are confronted with a similar set of circumstances.

PERU. A major educational reform is underway in Peru.[4] The "big dream" is beginning to materialize and detailed implementation planning is underway. Basically, this plan calls for decentralizing education into regions based on geographic and ethnic rather than existing political units of the country.

The plan calls for an educational cycle which encompasses secondary and junior college levels. This cycle of three or four years will be conducted in newly created "High Schools for Professional Education" which will place the emphasis on vocational training and work experience for all students. Graduates of these "high schools" will receive professional diplomas which qualify them either to enter employment or to continue on to the second cycle of higher education at a university.

Considering the classical and elitist traditions of education in South America, this is a bold plan. It gives emphasis to the types of programs offered in our community junior colleges and keeps the system "open." Like the development in Venezuela, it warrants watching. It could become a pattern for educational reform in South America.

COLOMBIA. Higher education in Colombia in recent years has been plagued by student unrest with many of the universities frequently being closed. A power struggle of rival political factions in the national congress and between faculties and administrators has minimized educational reform. There seems little likelihood that the structural changes will occur that are necessary to permit normal transfer from a junior college type institution to a

---

[4]Plan Nacional de Desarrollo 1971-1975. Vol. VIII. "Plan de Educacion," Ministerio de Educacion, Lima, Peru.

university. Some universities that undertook to develop credit units are considering discarding them due to faculty pressure. Consequently, it seems probable that the pattern in Colombia will continue to be that of technical institutes under direction of the Ministry of Education.

Several technical institutes have been opened in recent years. They offer occupational programs similar to those in American junior colleges but more limited in scope. Several have agricultural experimental farms. One technical institute with such a farm near Medellin helps local farmers improve their operations and makes available to them on a cost basis machinery owned and maintained by the institute. This institute also has an arrangement with a nearby university which enables some of its students to transfer.

An unusual and interesting educational unit in Colombia is the SENA (Servicio Educativo Nacional Aprendizaje) schools. There are 17 of these schools, operated by the Ministry of Labor, which offer vocational training in a wide range of fields. They are financed by an industrial payroll tax and operate independent of the Ministry of Education. These schools are the best financed of any public schools in Colombia. Their faculties are well qualified, and their programs well organized. If these SENA schools were extended to offer technical level programs, they would serve an important community college function.

Trends in Developed Countries

CANADA. In Canada, the term "community college" is used in a generic sense. It is applied to a group of institutions across the nation having certain features in common. None presently grant degrees and all are oriented in some way to their communities. Programs range from short courses to curricula requiring three years of study beyond high school. The majority of programs are one and two years in length. Most of the colleges are public institutions with an "open door" policy and low tuition (no tuition is charged in Quebec), while others are private institutions with selective admission and relatively high tuition. By definition, a *Canadian community college is a non-degree granting, post-secondary institution (public or private) which offers occupations and/or university parallel studies ranging in length from a few months to three years.* Within this definition, there were over 140 such colleges in 1972 with approximately 75 percent of them being public institutions.

Canada has had short-cycle, post-secondary institutions for some time. Eleven institutions classified as junior colleges existed in 1934; by 1959 the number had reached forty-nine. The major development, however, occurred after 1960.

Since education is the responsibility of each province in Canada, public community colleges vary substantially among the provinces. In Quebec they are broadly comprehensive institutions known as CEGEP's ("Colleges d'enseignement General et Professionel," i.e. colleges of general and vocational education). All university students must complete a CEGEP program before being admitted to a university. In addition, a wide range of occupational programs are offered. By contrast, in Ontario they offer only occupational programs and are known as CAAT's (Colleges of Applied Arts and Technology). There are also differences in the language of instruction. In Quebec and New Brunswick the majority of institutions teach in French, whereas instruction is in English in the remainder of the provinces.

Evidence of the growing role of importance which community colleges are playing in Canada was the formation in 1970 of the Association of Canadian Community Colleges.[5] It is an association of institutions created to coordinate, promote, and otherwise advance community college education in Canada.

AUSTRALIA. In Australia there are four types of institutions which offer short-cycle, post-secondary education programs. There are colleges of advanced education (about fifty), technical colleges (over 300), a number of teachers colleges, and agricultural colleges. The colleges of advanced education offer programs which characterize the other types of colleges identified above as well as programs offered by senior technical colleges, paramedical colleges, colleges of pharmacy, agricultural colleges, and schools of art and music. The programs of these colleges of advanced education vary greatly in length, some terminating with a diploma or certificate, while others lead to the baccalaureate and, in a few cases, the master's degree.

One Australian educator who is knowledgeable about higher education in the United States has expressed the view that Australia's colleges of advanced education will evolve into institutions similar to our state colleges and that their technical colleges will be the closest corollary to the American community colleges.

Of possible future significance in Australian post-secondary education is a community college being planned for Darwin in the North Territory. It is expected to open in 1974. Those who are planning it emphasize that Darwin Community College is not being modeled after any overseas institution but is drawing ideas from other countries whenever they have relevance for Darwin's needs. The chairman of the planning committee for the college states, "If it remains true to its original concept and if it has careful planning and good management, the college could be a forerunner of a new form of post-secondary education institutions in Australia."[6] It will be interesting to see the degree to which this institution resembles an American comprehensive community college.

[5] Further information about the Association can be obtained from Mr. Jacques Fournier, Executive Director, 845, Boul. Ste. Croix, St. Laurent Montreal, 379 Canada.

[6] H. G. Coughlin, "The Darwin Community College," *Education Now.* 12:20, August 1970, p. 7.

EUROPEAN COUNTRIES. An excellent analysis of trends in community college type education in western Europe, the Scandanavian countries, and Yugoslavia appears in a 1971 publication entitled *Towards New Structures of Post-Secondary Education* published in Paris by OECD (Organization for Economic Cooperation and Development).

The traditional European model for short-cycle post-secondary education has been the specialized institution with students coming from the non-academic streams of secondary education. In this respect they are a continuation of the streaming process begun at the secondary level. These institutions have the following characteristics: links with the university are largely non-existent, each institution offers a limited number of programs and specializes in a few areas, and they are centrally administered . from the regional or national level. (The reader will recall how closely these conditions apply to the technical institutes and colleges in the Asian and South American countries which were reviewed.)

During the late 1960's, a number of European countries began to introduce far-reaching reforms. These reforms can be classified under three models: the specialized model, the binary model, and the multi-purpose model. Examples of the *specialized model* are the "Enseignement Technique Superieur" in Belgium, the IUT's in France, reorganization of the "Fachhoch-schulen" in Germany, the polytechnics which are being planned in Portugal, and the overall higher education reform in Spain.

England's structure represents the *binary model*, which consists of dividing higher education into two separate sectors; the autonomous university sector, and the "advanced furthering education" sector which is highly diversified, serving many of the functions of American community junior colleges with part-time study, work-study arrangements, and adult evening courses.

The closest approximations to the United States *multi-purpose model* in Europe are found in Yugoslavia and Norway. Both have developed multi-purpose short-cycle institutions. Yugoslavia in the late 1950's and 1960's developed an extensive system of "Vise Skole," (two-year post-secondary institutions), offering both transfer and terminal programs. As of 1972, there were approximately 140 of these institutions. More recently, Norway opened three District Colleges with seven now in operation. They have many of the characteristics of American community junior colleges.

Additional information on recent development in various European countries is available from papers and reports prepared for OECD. These include the following:[7]

---

[7] These reports can be requested from the authors or from Dorotea Furth, OECD, 2, rue Andre-Pascal, Paris 16e, France.

1. *The Norwegian Regional Colleges*, Mr. Ingjold Ø. Sørheim, Head, Regional College Section, Ministry of Education, Oslo, Norway, October 1971.   DAS/EID/71.47

2. *Sweden: Planning New Structures of Post-Secondary Education*, November 1970.   DAS/EID/70.24/18

3. *Belgium: Planning New Structures of Post-Secondary Education*, March 1971   DAS/EID/70.24/03

4. *Spain: Planning New Structures of Post-Secondary Education*, November 1970.   DAS/EID/70.24/06

5. *Models of Short-Cycle Higher Education Envisaged in the Netherlands*, W.C.M. Van Lieshont, October 1971.   DAS/EID/71.70

6. *Germany: Planning New Structures of Post-Secondary Education*, November 1970.   DAS/EID/70.24/01

7. *Finland: Planning New Structures of Post-Secondary Education*, November 1970.   DAS/EID/70.24/22

8. *The Place and Role of IUT's In New French Universities*, J.L. Quermonne, October 1971.   DAS/EID/71.70

9. *Development of Two-Year Post-Secondary Schools in Yugoslavia*, Institute for Social Research, University of Zagreb.   DAS/EID/71.2

SUMMARY

There is every reason to expect that the trend toward the development of short-cycle higher education will continue. Even though factors such as a lack of financial resources, vested interests, and tradition may at times slow the trend, it will continue. The pressures of student numbers, the growing concept of viewing education in terms of utilization of human resources, manpower needs, and economic return; the push toward long-range comprehensive planning in education; and the movement away from elitist to mass education combine to produce a force that is not likely to be stopped.

The form which the new structures take is going to vary from country to country. In some cases it will probably closely resemble the American community junior college; in other cases, the British binary system, and some will continue to be specialized single purpose institutions. Whatever structure a particular country elects, however, American experience can be of value. Where there is a desire for our assistance, we can make contributions in the following ways.

American Universities which have graduate programs in community college administration, teaching, and curriculum development can serve graduate students from other countries who will return to positions of educational leadership. Our state agencies for community colleges and occupational education can offer internship experiences as can our community colleges and technical institutes to those who have responsibility for short-cycle higher education in other countries. American community colleges and technical institutes can offer teaching internship opportunities for faculty members who staff short-cycle institutes in other countries.

Our community college and technical institute administrators and faculty members can provide short and long-term technical assistance to other countries. Because of the differences in salaries, this will require either grants from funding agencies and/or the salary benefits of sabbatical leaves.

Agencies such as the World Bank, the Inter-American Development Bank, and the United States Agency for International Development can provide financial assistance for short-cycle higher education to countries which wish to develop and expand this segment of education. This, in turn, would provide the funds needed for the type of technical assistance referred to above.

We can share with educational leaders and policy makers in other countries American publications on community college and technical education which have relevance for them. Further, we can study the development of short-cycle post-secondary education of other countries as a means of acquiring insights that will enable us to improve the effectiveness of our institutions.

REFERENCES

Campbell, Gordon, *Community Colleges in Canada*. New York, McGraw-Hill Company, 1971.

Collins, Charles G. "Exporting the Junior College Idea" *In International Development of the Junior College*, R. Yarrington, ed., pp. 156-68. Washington, D.C., American Association of Junior Colleges, 1970.

Coughlin, H.G. "The Darwin Community College," *Education Now* (August, 1970) 7.

Do, Khe, Ba. "The Community College in Vietnam," *Junior College Journal* 42 (November, 1971) 16-19.

Education in Korea: Goals for the Year and Long-Range Plans. Seoul, Ministry of Education, Republic of Korea. 1971.

Innovations in Higher Education: Technical Education in the United Kingdom. Paris, France, Organization for Economic Cooperation and Development.

Innovations in Higher Education: Reforms in Yugoslavia. Paris, France, Organization for Economic Cooperation and Development.

Joshi, K.L. "The Junior College: Its Place in the Educational Structure," *University News* 12: (December 1971) 10-14.

Junior Colleges in Japan, 1971. Tokyo, Japan, Association of Private Junior Colleges, 1971.

Kandari, Abdul Ali. *A Junior College for Afghanistan.* Kabul, Afghanistan, Faculty of Education, University of Kabul, 1970.

"Plan de Educacion" In *Plan Nacional de Desarrollo*, 1971-1975, Vol. III. Lima, Peru, Ministerio de Educacion.

Toward New Structures of Post-Secondary Education. Paris, Organization for Economic Cooperation and Development, 1971.

Yarrington, Roger, ed. *International Development of the Junior College Idea.* Washington, D.C., American Association of Junior Colleges, 1970.

Chapter 7

INTERNATIONAL SCHOOLS, A Reflection

Robert J. Leach

In the summer of 1965, I attended the bi-annual meeting of the Council for Internationally-Minded Schools, held in part at Colorado Academy in Denver, Colorado. In attendance, representing the United States State Department, was James A. Donovan, Jr., Staff Director of the U.S. Advisory Commission on International Education and Cultural Affairs. The year 1965 had marked the creation of that body, now known as the International Baccalaureate Office (IBO), which was incorporated under Swiss law, and affiliated with UNESCO as a category B, private, international organization. As I was the Chairman of the Executive Committee of IBO at the time, Donovan was interested in exploring common fields of interest with me.

Perhaps I should indicate here that the International Baccalaureate is an internationally administered university entrance examination which allows secondary school graduates to enter practically every important university in the world. Its level is roughly that of the Advanced Placement Programme of the College Entrance Examination Board. In my book,[1] I trace the rise of IBO, which began in my own Social Studies Department at the International School of Geneva.

In short, Jim Donovan found himself talking, perhaps for the first time in his life, to a man who self-consciously and intentionally has promoted multi-lateral internationalism in the field of education. What these rather pretentious words really signify is an educational programme not copied from any national system, but incorporating some of the best elements of a number of them, and administered by boards of managers, no one of which may be dominated by the nationals of one country. In fact, the boards of multi-lateral international organizations must be set up so that each group of national appointees acts in minority to the whole.

Technical aid funds were channeled to overseas schools serving American nationals through U.S. Public Law 480. Donovan fully admitted that these schools only qualified for such aid (normally) if the State Department was convinced that the schools adequately prepared students to enter colleges and universities in the United States and, if they were in fact, generally under the preponderant influence of the American Ambassadors accredited to the countries in which they were located. It is perfectly understandable that the State Department should be interested in assuring that the offspring of

---

[1] *International Schools and their Role in the Field of Internation Education*, Oxford, Pergamon, 1969

overseas American diplomatic personnel be given educational opportunities roughly equal to those found "state-side." But it does seem less attractive that certain genuinely international schools in a good many places have been forced to split up or slough off non-American participation in order to attract U.S. dollars. This procedure, seemed to me all the more absurd, as the College Entrance Examination Board programme hardly qualifies any student to enter any institution other than a university in the United States or possibly Canada.

In 1961-1962, I visited schools of an international character on three continents (twenty-six countries). I was distressed to find that the greatest potential catalysing force as far as genuine multi-lateral internationalism was concerned in overseas education (namely the U.S. State Department) had, if anything, about the worst record of any element in the picture. It would appear that Americans had become the most ardent ethnocentrically-oriented nationalists in our supposedly international twentieth century. Of course, this was a false image, for the U.S.S.R. maintains a string of ethnocentrically-run overseas schools. You can be sure that on March 1st in each school each student will be learning data from the same book and even on the same page as his peer in Leningrad, Moscow or Kiev!

"American International Schools," as they are quite openly called, are nowhere near so nationalistic. They welcome nationals of other countries, not only those of the NATO grouping. In fact they serve as "demonstration centers" of American education. But in the final analysis, they open higher education doors in America or in U.S. institutions abroad, just as the Russian schools do for universities in the Soviet Union.

Rather naturally the French have set up a chain of Lycees, particularly in the Francophone or French-speaking world. These rather superior institutions open doors in France at the university level. Parallel to these are the schools run by the British Council for Anglophone entrance into British universities. The Germans, Spaniards, – even the Turks do a parallel job. The only major difference between the American Overseas School and the Swedish Overseas School, generally speaking, is that there are many more of the first type. Neither contributes substantially to the international ideal, to which the United Nations at least gives lip service.

Such ethnocentric nationalism in overseas education constituted the "windmill" against which "Don Quixote" Leach tilted his lance in 1965 by helping to organize the International Baccalaureate Office. Donovan had the kindness and I would also add, the good sense, to recognize that what we were undertaking in Geneva should be of interest to the U.S. Government. In short, he saw to it that I was invited to a Conference on Education for International Understanding held at Airlie House, Warrenton, Virginia, by the Wemyss and Airlie Foundations on 1-3 April, 1966, at the encouragement of the White House. In fact two Special Assistants to President Johnson attended, along with several well known educators, and some members of Congress and the State Department. I should note that this was a unilateral international conference. Everyone was a U.S. citizen concerned with looking at international education from a stateside approach.

About a month before this conference, Education and World Affairs, a Ford-Rockefeller subsidiary, had published a pamphlet which introduced a congressional bill entitled the "International Education Act of 1966." The act, which was endorsed by President Lyndon Johnson on 2 February, 1966, called for 56 million dollars yearly for a State Department cultural and education program. This act allowed grants to be made for the first time to institutions not controlled by a national of the United States.

I should point out that the first grant of $300,000 from the Ford Foundation to finance the IBO programme came in part as a result of counsel given to Ford by Education and World Affairs. In the spring of 1964 I was asked to present the original idea of IBO to the American Foundation World and subsequently received $75,000 from the Twentieth Century Fund, since I had continuously put forward the importance of a neutral stance in international education. I can only surmise that a reasonable idea found response from other reasonable minds. Possibly I was a catalytic agent at that time.

However, as with other aspects of the nearly forgotten "great society," Johnson's International Education Act, which was passed by Congress some weeks later, remained a dead letter. No concurrent appropriation was ever passed, and the hopes of the Airlie House Conference, some of them political and even professional, were dashed.

I should prehaps recall that the Airlie House Conference was dominated by such luminaries as Marshall MacLuhan and Harold Taylor. I also addressed the conference regarding what we were carrying out in Geneva, noting that the International School of Geneva was so constitutionally set up that it could adequately serve as the laboratory for testing the International Baccalaureate. In neither case was it possible for the American expatriate community, though dominant in numbers, nor the U.S. Government, to exert more than a consultative influence.

As I had lived sixteen years abroad, had married a British wife, and had learned to speak French fluently, my own spoken word did not reflect current American educational lingo. In any case I was listened to not only with great attention, but with a certain amazement. It never occurred to most of those present that it was possible, still less desirable, to consider international education from any other stance than an American-based (ethnocentric) position. I make no pretence that I won converts. But I probably helped open some hitherto unimagined vistas. It is because of this Airlie House experience that I am willing, perhaps even eager, to write this essay.

In the *Year Book of Education*, entitled "Education and International Life" (Evans Brothers, London, 1964, published jointly by Columbia and London Universities), I contributed a chapter entitled "International Secondary Schools."[2] I set out at that time to classify international schools according to their internationalism, technically speaking. I think I still adhere to the categories therein enumerated, though the mutual absorption of the Council of Internationally Minded-Schools by the International Schools Association blurs distinctions somewhat. In this essay, however, I am not concerned to rehash what I wrote in 1964 nor even in 1969, but rather to put down, as the editor of this book most charmingly put it, "the philosophies, nature, differences, excitement and other important aspects of these unique educational institutions," *viz.*, international schools.

Among the Airlie House attenders was Mrs. Dorothy Goodman, Headmistress and Founder of the Washington International School. As wife of an official in the World Bank and a friend of Robert McNamara, Mrs. Goodman has done the impossible in creating the second international school in the U.S.A. with Ford Foundation help. Ford does not help needy schools, but it is alert to unique educational opportunity. Where else but in Washington (in the U.S.A.) may children of the inner city receive education along side children of diplomats from the emergent nations of Africa? How better to recover a lost heritage? Only a month ago Dorothy Goodman passed through Geneva. Her school is now developing its secondary section. It needs to build its curriculum into the International Baccalaureate programme. Here-in lies part of the excitement.

The United Nations International School of New York pioneered in offering the first full programme International Baccalaureate (IB) candidates in 1970. At least two IB candidates from the United Nations school transferred to other international schools, where they completed their two year IB studies. One of these is now a freshman at Princeton. This boy, a gifted citizen of India, gave a great deal to the Theory of Knowledge Course, which is required of all graduates in his second school. Unlike many national educational systems which emphasize content of courses, the IB stresses epistomology; i.e., knowing how we know in each discipline. Here again is excitement and philosophy in practice.

A few weeks ago I was in Sevres at the French Pedagogical Institute, which is housed in Mme. de Pompadour's pottery. There in 1956 the European Baccalaureate was approved as it is currently prepared for by the six Common Market Schools. There at Sevres, in 1967, the International Baccalaureate was approved by representatives of a good many more nations, including Bulgaria and Poland. This year, panels of historians and geographers from participating

---

[2] Michael Knight and Robert Leach, "International Secondary Schools" *In Education and International Understanding: Yearbook of Education*, pp. 443-457. London, Evans Brothers Limited, 1964.

schools and examination boards were assembled to discuss their IB syllabi.

The International Baccalaureate consists of six subjects, three at Higher Level, and three at Lower Level, in addition to the "Theory of Knowledge" course. Five areas of work must be covered in a six subject spread. These include working language, foreign language, mathematics, laboratory science, and science of man. We were concerned at Sevres with the last area, partly to establish a "Culture of Cities" Course. The only sensible way to do this, short of hiring specialists, is for each international school to develop units in the history, geography and economics of its home city. All this winter our three departments held in-service-training sessions on Geneva, producing three units complete with audio-visual aids, which we demonstrated at Sevres. It now appears that the International Schools of Tehran, Iran, Ibadan, Nigeria, and Copenhagen, Denmark, are most likely to produce similar materials for us to exchange, so that the course dealing with two cities (or three) may begin in the autumn of 1973. Obviously teachers' conferences stimulate the cross-fertilization of ideas. But does any cities course in the United States deal with cities found outside American boundaries, using appropriate units prepared by international teams in each city?

Geneva is an old aristocratic republic overlaid by an international clientele. Tehran is a modern artificial desert capital, flooded by peasants and pollution. Ibadan is an old native black city, recapturing and translating the exceedingly coveted mores of the Yoruba tribe. Copenhagen is the bridge between Europe and Scandinavia, erotically free, but culturally frightfully provincial. As most people in our world will live in cities in the next generation, it would seem to be appropriate to train up people to understand their environment.

One of the strange ironies of Europe is that its great capitals generally boast no international schools. The International School of Paris is really a French-owned and managed private school, although an ex-NATO school at St. Germain-en-Laye does prepare for the International Baccalaureate, as does the Lycee connected with the Pedagogical Institute at Sevres. Here the trouble is two-fold. National overseas schools, like the American School of Paris, are well established. And the French Government, though it recognizes the IB, insists that French nationals living in France take the French Baccalaureate.

Once again it would seem clear that personal contact as much as anything else helps to spread multi-lateral internationalism. This is certainly true in the involvement of the World College of the Atlantic in Wales, which is now developing sister institutions in western Canada and in Singapore. Atlantic College, which brings students from all over the world on scholarship to an "outward bound" type of sixth form experience, presented its first full IB candidates in 1971, along with us in Geneva. Again the unique quality of the Atlantic College programme originally attracted Ford Foundation money, but like the International Baccalaureate Office, Atlantic College now gets money from many foundations the world over.

In 1971, over 600 candidates were present at International Baccalaureate examinations, seventy-six of whom sat the full diploma; fifty-four passed. Twelve preparatory schools entered candidates. These are listed according to the number of candidates presented: Atlantic College (Wales), Lycee Internationale (St. Germain-en-Laye), U.N.I.S. (New York), Iranzamin (Tehran), British Schools (Montevideo), Ibadan (Nigeria), Geneva (Switzerland), Lycee Pilote (Sevres), Copenhagen (Denmark), International College (Beirut), Frankfurt (Germany), National College of Cheusifat (Lebanon).

It is the intention of IBO to maintain participation in the International Baccalaureate to a manageable minimum until 1975, when it is hoped that UNESCO will incorporate the programme as part of its own world-wide activities. Then it will be more possible for schools universally to opt for at least some subject examinations. There is of course the possibility that the extreme nationalism of some UNESCO members may prevent this incorporation of IBO, at least for some years.

It should be pointed out that the League of Nations consistently refused to have anything to do with education except to sponsor a comparative programme in the International Bureau of Education. To date, UNESCO has remained relatively inactive regarding genuine multi-lateral international education, except to sponsor both the International Schools Association and the International Baccalaureate.

In looking back over the dozen schools presenting IB candidates in 1971, attention has been drawn in this essay to the first three. In checking over the succeeding nine, it is apparent that only one is located in a European capital. Bonn, Brussels, The Hague, Rome, Lisbon, Madrid, Vienna, Belgrade, Athens, Oslo, Stockholm and Bern, to note others, are missing. At least eight of these capitals boast a primary grade international school and/or an American International secondary school. If these are bound together in any way, it will be normally through the European Council of International Schools, an American affiliate of the International Schools Foundation of Washington, D.C. (in turn an associate of the State Department). What the European Council of International Schools and the International Schools Foundation strive for is to assure that stateside know-how, personnel and accreditation are made available to American oriented overseas schools, particularly in Europe (though the International Schools Foundation has a wider parish).

Last year I served on a Middle States Association accrediting team sent to the Rome Overseas School. There I had an opportunity to draw the International Baccalaureate programme to the attention of both the School's administrative staff and the accrediting committee. As an increasing number of graduates from the Rome School attended European universities, to which they cannot be admitted by College Entrance Examination Board tests, the good sense of the IB programme recommends itself. However, since the International Baccalaureate is not necessary for entrance into American universities, and the Rome School thinks only in such terms, even the recommendation made by the accrediting committee that the Rome School look into IB possibilities made minimal impression. The attitude of the Rome School is that any student opting for a European university should attend St. Stephens British School, or if bilingual, the Lycee de Chateaubriand, both of which qualify students for European universities. The same mentality obtains for most American high schools outside continental United States.

The result of such an approach is that most American educators and pupils abroad find themselves in an essentially American ghetto, for mingling with non-Americans is minimal, except in an American-based programme. It is possible for U.S. citizens to live many years abroad without having learned to put themselves into the shoes of their host neighbors, to say nothing of other national groupings also guests like themselves. Not only has the U.S. Government promoted ethnocentrism for American nationals abroad, but the overseas schools provide for this approach — largely because it is familiar, easy to carry out, and avoids questioning items as familiar as "God, Mother and the Girl Scouts" as the saying puts it.

The International School of Frankfort, as well as that in Copenhagen, is essentially American inspired. But they are both run by administrators who have grasped the wider sense of opportunity which the International Baccalaureate offers. The same comment applies to the school in Montevideo, except that its British director understands its usefulness. The school in Ibadan and the two in the Lebanon reveal more complicated situations in which two developing nations wish to find a satisfactory educational system, free of the overtones of one-time colonialism. The Tehran School was founded by an American headmaster who welcomed the approach of multi-lateral internationalism when I first met him there in 1962. His international school exists within a traditional authoritarian monarchy of an Islamic complexion — this naturally poses the problem of cultural confrontation. That this school is flourishing pays tribute to Richard Irvine's vision and perseverance — as well as the relevance of the true international ideal in a complicated situation. I should perhaps add that for those who want it, there are two American secondary schools in the Iranian capital.

The old adage that "a prophet is without honor in his own country" applies to my own situation in Geneva. Dr. Fred Redefer of New York University has called attention in various publications to anomalies in the Geneva situation. Martin Mayer in his book *Diploma* (New York, Twentieth Century Fund, 1966) has more pertinent data to add.

I should like at this point to insist, as we all realize in our better moments, that all schools, teachers, programmes and movements flag on occasion. To be successful requires an ever increasing tempo of exciting innovation. There is a limit to this tempo, short of nervous breakdown. There are also insoluble problems which can only be outlived. Perhaps the most difficult problem involving multi-lateral international education is to find an effective administrator. He must be a genius in a number of situations in which the interplay of subliminal national values vie with each other, though nothing in his national training, nor often in his previous practical professional experience equips him to deal with such situations. It is difficult to find a Secretary General for the United Nations. It is no easier for the genuinely international school; and there is no salary compatibility between the two jobs.

Thus the International School of Geneva still suffers from being divided into an English-speaking and French-speaking section. It still suffers from too much Swiss influence, too many American parents, and too many British staff. It has, notwithstanding, manifested some helpful signs. It has become joint owner of a campus on the right bank of the Rhone and Lake, which is used by the Lycee des Nations. It has been the recipient of a ten million Swiss franc loan at 2½% from the Republic of Geneva. This is to be matched with other money in a rebuilding programme. It shares with the United Nations International School in the proceeds of a United Nations stamp issue. The original design was donated by Picasso. It has built an experimental theater workshop through which drama has become a city-wide institution.

It is important to realize that practically all teachers and administrators are products of national systems. Our International School of Geneva will be fifty years old next year. International education is only that old. Our school boasts one alumna in the figure of Indira Gandhi. What will we have a quarter century from now? And what will other international schools produce? Education is often considered the dullest of subjects by the uninstructed layman. It is not the case if we work actively for the realization of the "Eosphere" of which Teilhard de Chardin wrote. The global village is a realizable ideal.

REFERENCES

Knight, Michael and Robert Leach. "International Secondary Schools" In *Education and International Understanding* Yearbook of Education, pp. 443-457. London, Evans Brothers Limited, 1964.

Leach, Robert J. *International Schools and Their Role in Field of International Education*. Oxford, Pergamon Press, 1969.

Mayer, Martin. *Diploma*. New York, Twentieth Century Fund, 1966.

Part II

ROLES OF OVERSEAS AMERICAN EDUCATORS

In the past, direct interaction between Americans and other peoples of the world in their home countries primarily included only missionaries, military men, statesmen, and businessmen. Now, the American tourist, especially the young one, and especially in the summer, can be found from the Tower of London to the beaches of eastern Australia. American students attend academic classes abroad in both replicas of their own schools at home and foreign educational institutions. And with them come their mentors, elementary and secondary school teachers, principals, superintendents, college and university academics and administrators.

Not only does the overseas American educational contingent include teachers and administrators; additionally, there are researchers, educational consultants in all fields, librarians, dormitory supervisors, counselors, evaluators, and government officials involved in educational missions. Many are on independent projects, but most work in American, international or dependent schools or overseas college and university branches. Some are employed by such organizations as UNESCO or AID. A few are on the staffs of foreign schools or educational government agencies.

In looking at American education overseas, we must view the work of the U.S. educators abroad and the seeds and fruits of their endeavors. It is difficult to select from among them to do proper justice to the extent and value of their experiences to themselves and to others, both American and foreign. However, to insure at least a little variety in both roles and geographical locations in which overseas American educators are found, the following professionals were asked to contribute articles: a former superintendent of schools in Monrovia, Liberia; a private college administrator who taught in a Kenyan higher educational institution; an American currently serving on the faculty of an Australian university; a former teacher of English as a Second Language who retired after a pleasurable tour of employment for the American University in Cairo; the principal of the Canadian Academy in Kobe, Japan; a university faculty member and administrator who specializes in Latin American education and has frequently served as a consultant to foreign governments and educational organizations; and a comparative educationalist whose expertise is in European education.

They provide observations and advice. Consistently, they use their own experiences to point out conditions and pitfalls which those who anticipate following in their overseas footstep might take under thoughtful consideration.

Thomas Kelly writes about schools which primarily educate American children overseas. He shares some of the concerns upon which administrators far away from their homeland must seriously reflect. He squarely opines what American-curriculum schools abroad are and are not. He addresses some of the many problems encountered: transiency, curriculum, financing, and distance. He touches briefly on the benefits of the School-to-School program. He also suggests many of the essential tools which the educational craftsman should have for his foreign venture.

In escorting the reader through a selected set of incidents in his own sojourn at a teacher training college in Africa, Thomas Quinlan honestly evaluates the plight and the privileges of the expatriate teacher. His is almost a case study of the advocates of two greatly differing philosophies of education meeting head-on in a country searching for its own essential theories and solutions concerning education. He openly shares his impressions with descriptions of specific incidents which he encountered and his own reactions to them. His narrative style accompanies a series of dramatic situations. Dr. Quinlan does place his observations in a broader prospective and does look forward with optimism.

Dennis Buckley, who has also spent a number of years teaching in German schools, is (at this writing) teaching at Riverina College in New South Wales, Australia. His unique approach to his article allows one to look at several of the realistic features of assimilating into a new educational environment, in a new country, with new colleagues. His delightful essay is spiked with anecdotal incidents that his first hand impressions freshly reveal. His work "down-under" provides an "up-over" observation of an American attempting to settle down like an Indian swami over a pit of hot coals.

Another role of Americans overseas is to help adapt certain U.S. curricular programs for foreign consumption. Not only is such influence permeating many foreign elementary and secondary schools, but it is also present in higher education. An excellent example is described by Blase Donadio. He has selected English as a Second Language as the program illustration and the Middle East as the overseas recipient. He is quite familiar with both. He considers the aura of mystique which many foreigners admit having about Americans and the United States, and the many factors which prevent them from learning adequately under our methods and techniques particularly when we do not give proper consideration to those with which they are more familiar.

With Al Chudler, one can place himself in the chair and in the active involvements of an administrator who has the responsibility for insuring that American youth, several thousand miles away from their native country, receive a proper education. He provides a prospective of the educational decision maker who must look at the situation of an overseas school in the light of specific and unique problems and issues which are particular to such schools. His helpful insights into the actualities of what a principal faces overseas provide a set of rare exposures to the special issues of the transposed administrator.

Thomas LaBelle provides an historical approach to the evolution of education in Latin America and the impact of foreign colonial nations. He points to the French, Iberian and Spanish influences on the Latin American educational systems. He summarizes the technical and financial assistance of which such countries are recipients. He provides a helpful analysis of what expertise actually includes as an overseas educational consultant. Uniquely, he views American educational practice as an exportable item, along with the movement of once dependent nations toward their own independence.

Val Rust, who specializes in European education, provides insights on educational change in three different patterns overseas which have major implications for educational reform in American schools, both here and abroad. His chapter is included in this section as a reminder that educators preparing to teach, administrate, or perform other functions and tasks overseas *must* be aware of what happens in the educational systems of other countries, particularly in those in which they serve. He reinforces the concept of a teacher having the responsibility of being a change agent, an educational reformer, a participant in change with others, and a leader. He highlights features of foreign systems which he views as innovative. Hopefully, these selected roles of American educators evidence a cast of characters whose individual influence on education in an international context is extremely significant.

To serve youth as well as the interests of American or foreign governmental or school officials or idealists overseas is a great responsibility for any educator. The overseas professional is not clothed with the protection of a local, state, or national educational entity and the stability (usually) of an involved and knowledgeable broad or governing agency of trustees, a dedicated and concerned faculty and staff, and students who reside in the culture in which they are to be educated. The overseas professional has to count greatly on his own self-reliance.

Chapter 8

THE OVERSEAS SCHOOL: ADMINISTRATIVE
CREATIVITY PUT TO THE TEST

Thomas F. Kelly

Perhaps it may appear too basic or even naive, but the first question an American educator considering an overseas assignment must seriously put to himself is "Why do I want to go abroad?" The answer is crucial, not only in deciding whether or not to go, but more importantly, to consider what kind of assignment to seek. There are any number and variety of opportunities and each one may call for an entirely different motivation. Those desiring to interact with educators of another culture might well find themselves applying for a position in a foreign country's school system or as advisors to Ministries of Education. Those wishing to travel overseas had better think and explore hard and long because the opportunity to travel may be limited to the trip from home overseas to the job overseas and back again. The choice must be made before accepting any overseas assignment or the experience could be devastating. In short, much pre-thought and investigation must occur since the assignment is rarely what it may have appeared to have been from afar and time for adjustment is minimal.

This chapter will be devoted exclusively to comments about schools established with the permission of the host country but designed to primarily meet the needs of American dependents. An understanding of this definition is essential because the educator must plan to implement programs of American standards and quality within an environment that does not readily provide the means for easily accomplishing the goals of an American-type school. This is not to imply that there will necessarily be conflict, but rather that one must be sensitive to the cultural aspirations of host country nationals. Such recognition is a prime prerequisite for the smooth functioning of an American in a foreign setting. It is precisely herein that the main challenge lies in this type of education. How does one develop an American program without interfering with the sovereignty and integrity of the local educators? The idealist may find it easy to envision, from his position in the States, the unlimited potential for capitalizing upon the local environment. However, upon arriving at the overseas post he may find that some of his idealism will dissipate as he discovers that the school is fundamentally no different from the school he is familiar with at home. He may be quick to see that the only operational difference between an American school in Trenton and Trieste is that they are located in different cities.

Why, indeed then, should an educator leave the known for the unknown if his function will be the same? Be assured that much will be the same —

budgetary problems, curriculum revision, in-service education, recruiting, textbook selection, capital improvement, maintenance, long hours, shortened vacations, and an amelioration of divergent parent opinions regarding the operation of the school. Very simply put, the lure of the overseas school is the potential it offers to the creative administrator. Freed from the shackles of bureaucratic red-tape that often inhibits education, the overseas leader has the unlimited opportunity to provide exciting education within the bounds of few constraints. He will not miss State and Federal laws, pressure groups lobbying for the imposition of their interests, court cases, social upheaval and the school being the whipping boy for current political and emotional extremes. It can provide every opportunity to put his professional expertise to the test.

How is this possible? By and large, the selection process that chooses parents for overseas assignments eliminates many of the special kinds of students that Stateside schools must provide for. Such a statement may sound condescending but in point of fact it merely states an observable situation. Children with special physical or emotional needs cannot always be cared for in the foreign environment. They are screened out, not because of prejudice, not because they are not wanted, but because the means are not at hand to help them. As a result, a homogenous population is enrolled. Accordingly, the programming of studies need not be as diverse nor as complex as in the States. On the other hand, the educational potential of the enrolled students is so high that proper planning to meet their needs requires creativity and imagination.

For the most part, overseas schools tend to be small. Interpersonal relationships are close. Opportunities abound for teamwork and for entire staffs to actively participate in decision-making. The absence of large administrative hierarchies enables everyone to contribute to the direction of the school. Student input is easy and natural. The net result is that administrative leadership can become meaningful and pleasurable; there is no need for fiats from the front office.

It would be misleading to imply that there are no problems or crises. They do exist; yet they differ greatly in kind from those in the States. Most of them are created by the transient nature of staff, board members, and students. The school administrator becomes more like a bus driver who picks up new passengers and lets old ones off at every stop, before he, himself, is relieved of duty. I have found that the foremost problem is coping with the inordinate but expected turnover of personnel. This causes a lack of continuity. When an administrator can hire staff locally, he is most fortunate. Permanence provides the stability evolving educational programs must have.

Generally, the chief administrator himself signs a two-year contract. This allows hardly enough time to do much more than prepare for a few innovative improvements. Usually, it will take most of the first year to develop rapport, identify needs, and begin to implement needed change. During the second year, as programming successfully develops, the tour of duty ends and the leader leaves. It is inherently evident that some method must be discovered to keep key people for a longer period of time. Importing teachers is no less a problem. Quite often, it is when they are leaving that their potential is finally realized. It becomes essential that a basic common philosophy of education is agreed upon and that all employees subscribe totally to that philosophy. If, every two years, the program changes according to the beliefs of the changing personnel, nothing but chaos will result.

With some Boards of Education changing completely each year, many schools have tried having semi-annual elections so there will always be an overlapping of Board membership. However, this system involves the school in perpetual campaigning and voting. For administrators who have faced the spectre of never-changing Boards, the prospect of a new Board each year can sound appealing. Unfortunately, however, short tenure often genders only a short term urgency for Board members to see their particular proposals implemented while they are still in office rather than addressing long term needs. I have worked with four different Boards of Education in three and a half years in the same school system. Each Board saw its function or prime emphasis in a slightly different way. It is fine to assume that if a Board restricts itself to merely setting policy no problems should accrue. The difficulty arises as each Board re-evaluates and changes past policy so that its implementation becomes rapid, confusing, and complicated.

At least one-third of the student population changed annually where I was located, as parents were reassigned to new posts. Their tours of duty were normally between two and three years. Behavioral needs of students differ. Additionally, some elements of familiarity, permanence, or consistency must be provided even amidst predictable instability. Students come from and go to a wide variety of educational systems. It becomes the school's role to accommodate these varying needs. Schedules, course offerings, time sequences, counseling procedures, and class requirements must somehow be adjustable to receiving students from American systems in the fifty States and throughout the world, as well as those who arrive from the English tutorial or French-speaking programs. At the same time, students must be capable of entering an equally infinite variety of schools anywhere in the world. Here is an example. Arriving at your school at the same time may be (1) a student who has been taught one or two years of French in traditional book fashion, but can speak very little of the language; (2) a student who has had one or two years of audio-lingual instruction, but can't read or write a word of French; and (3) a student who has lived in a Francophone country for two or three years, is almost bi-lingual in the vernacular, but knows little of the formal written or spoken language. They all want to continue in French for college preparation. How do you organize your French class for them? Will your language lab help? Do you have a lab? Can you use one if you don't have the teachers who know how to use it? Such complexities might be resolved if students were to remain for some time in the school, but in a short time they will be off to a new country or State. It is distressing to lack the flexibility to adapt to such students' needs. Some Stateside schools receiving students from overseas have greatly impeded their progress by imposing requirements which the student could not have fulfilled elsewhere. I know of one student who didn't meet his home State's physical education requirement and had to be held back to complete it. He had previously attended school in the tropics where physical activity was deemed inappropriate because of the intense heat and high humidity.

Also caught in this maelstrom is the student who comes abroad from a special, accelerated, innovative or experimental program — call it what you will — in a Stateside school. There appears to be a great influx of this type of student. Non-graded programs, flexible programs, computer assisted instruction, mini-courses and all the latest concepts may have untold value. Yet the values of such methods are predicated on the supposition that the student will remain in that particular school or can transfer to others which provide similar options. We received a seventeen-year-old student as a high school senior. As a sixth grader, he had been identified by his school district as gifted. He had been rightfully placed in an accelerated program. Upon his arrival at our school, we learned that he had already completed everything our school offered other than some elective courses which had nothing to do with aiding in his desired progression towards college. In fact, we found that probably the only school in the world which could provide him the opportunity to properly advance was his original school, where a special accelerated twelfth grade program was offered for those in their gifted program. We recommended his direct matriculation to college. He was not accepted because he had not completed high school!

Answers to such problems, of course, must come from more individually prescribed educational programming. Yet, finding and retaining administrators, teachers, and parents who are willing to live with individualization is no mean task. Transient parents see in the school one element of permanence in their transient lives. The school that tries to meet individual needs by special programming tends to deviate from the apparent stability of the lock-step system that parents see as an essential element of security. Attempts at non-gradedness, IGE, IPI, etc., have met with strong resistance and have often failed since they require stability and long-term planning — elements not often found in an overseas school.

Attempts at diversification are also limited by cost factors. Financial capability is the major drawback in planning the overseas operation. The shipping cost of an educational item can exceed the price of the item ordered. Income is derived primarily from tuition. Though turnover is anticipated, it is never accurately predictable. There is no precise method of knowing how many students will be in school from year to year. Thus, in any given September, the administrator has planned for an unknown number of students who are to be placed in unknown levels of learning. He has no detailed knowledge of his income until the first week of school when he has his first approximation of enrollment. A sudden change of American governmental policy or business transactions in a given year could spell disaster. With no direct pipeline to Congress, there is no way of knowing whether defense or foreign aid spending will be increased or decreased. Such spending has a direct effect upon the numbers of Americans assigned to a specific post. One overseas school with a tuition rate of $1,000 per year lost 400 students one summer. Imagine how you must re-adjust to 400 fewer students and $400,000 less in your anticipated budget!

Due to the distances involved, planning, recruiting of staff, and Stateside ordering of equipment and materials must be completed months in advance. If guesses are wrong, the wrong number of teachers and amount of supplies will be on hand and there will be no money to pay for either. Most administrators must face this dilemma by estimating income conservatively, budgeting expenses generously, and maintaining a large contingency reserve. They must also recruit people who are skilled and versatile. Elementary teachers must be prepared to teach at various, or even combined, grade levels; while secondary teachers must expect as many as five completely different subject preparations. Teachers find, however, that class sizes are usually very small, discipline problems are minimal, and students fit within a narrow, but high, range of abilities.

While distance from the States necessitates considerable long-term planning, isolation promotes quick recovery from routine problems. If a teacher, for one reason or another, must leave in the middle of the year, there is no colleague available at the other end of the phone who can give a quick lead to a good replacement. Even the absence of fellow administrators with whom to share ideas is a strange and unanticipated void. What could be a simple error easily rectified at home can be a major problem to an isolated school. A purchase order for books with the omission of the author's name brought us thirty of the wrong algebra books arriving one week before school began. No quick call to a salesman or a nearby district was possible. A re-order and a three month delay was the penalty. A flexible teacher who was not book-bound improvised until the books arrived.

Though instability of staff and isolation have their disadvantages, stability and permanence, though rare in overseas schools, create different problems. With a permanent staff, the school may lose the potential growth available through stateside in-service training programs conducted by districts, counties, states, or universities. New techniques of Stateside schools are shared by teachers coming abroad as they gather socially and professionally. These individualized opportunities are lost to the teacher residing permanently overseas, or to a staff which does not benefit from the flow of new and talented educational blood. The administrator, too, may find that he has lost out not only in seniority and tenure, but no longer has contact with those who might help him find another position upon re-entry in the U.S. A long-term commitment to the overseas school can quickly outdate him and continue a cycle of increasing mediocrity.

To overcome such built-in weaknesses, many schools are benefiting from the School-to-School program wherein a stateside system enters into a partnership with an overseas school. Properly executed, the overseas school can become a virtual extension — overseas campus, if you will — of the stateside system. Personnel can be exchanged without impairment of tenure; purchasing arrangements that are mutually beneficial can be arranged; teaching materials can be exchanged, as can cross-cultural experiences. Care must be taken, however, to preserve the uniquenesses of both the overseas school and the stateside district. Overseas schools should not become administrative units of stateside districts. They have different needs and different goals.

The administrator who recognizes and minimizes his dependence upon stateside partnership arrangements is not dependent on others far from him. True innovation involves drawing on the past, dealing honestly in the present, and planning, with excitement, for the future. The potential for future excellence should serve as a lure to the creative leader.

Only serious study can isolate and permit definition of the behaviorial needs peculiar to the overseas student. He is isolated from so many of the traditional American experiences so closely allied with American education. There are few interscholastic activities; social events are limited; television may be non-existent; and the freedom granted by the automobile is absent. Transiency may find him unable to know teachers well enough to obtain letters of recommendation for college entry. In fact, the whole college-going syndrome is exacerbated by the fact that overseas parents are, by and large, college graduated. Most view college as the singularly most important goal for their children. They encourage the cognitive approach because, in it, they see high scores on the Scholastic Aptitude Tests and ease of college acceptance. Thus, affective learning is difficult for the administrator to sell, particularly among diplomatic personnel and Department of Defense officials whose lives are dominated by memoranda and orders from higher authorities. Individualization may be looked upon askance by those adhering slavishly to chains of command.

All of us must pay greater attention to the problems of the overseas child who has never planted any roots. It is difficult for him to identify with the American culture as he moves from post to post, never having been in the States long enough to feel that he belongs. The role of the school in bridging that gap becomes paramount. Building such a bridge is possible only by capitalizing on the diversity of student, parent, and staff backgrounds, and through utilizing the cultural differences and similarities of the local scene to better understand the complexities of American life.

Creative overseas administrators can unleash the potentials of overseas schools in exciting, beneficial ways. Such accomplishment, however, requires a kitbag of educator-workman tools, each of which must be used at the proper moment of construction. Such tools include spontaneity; adaptability to change; adjustment to the foreign culture; sensitivity to and understanding of people different in attitudes, values and experiences, whether Americans or otherwise; and a keen sense of humor. Above all, to be successful, the overseas administrator should be a humanist, process rather than content oriented. Only with such tools can overseas educational programs be built to meet the very special needs of very special American children.

Chapter 9

AMERICAN AND BRITISH EXPATRIATE CONFLICTS IN AN AFRICAN TEACHER TRAINING INSTITUTION: A SELF-INDULGENT LUXURY

Thomas E. Quinlan

Kenyatta College, a constituent college of the University of Nairobi, is the major institution preparing secondary school teachers in Kenya. With over 1,000 students in 1971, 250 teachers were graduated that year as compared to a combined output of less than 100 from the University Education Department and the Kenya Science Teachers' College. Located approximately twelve miles from Nairobi on the Thika Road, the compound, a former British army base, also houses most of the college staff.

The college officially opened in 1964, and was described shortly thereafter as follows:

> The chief development which has taken place in the field of teacher training in Kenya during the last fifteen months is the opening of Kenyatta College. . . This college is housed in one part of the large compound which formerly housed British troups. . . The Ministry of Education has centralized on this site all training of secondary school teachers (non-graduate) for Kenya.

Two years later (December, 1967) the College was reorganized administratively and Mr. Shadrack Kimalel was appointed Principal and in 1969 a four year degree program was introduced.

The primary responsibility of the College lies in the training of local teachers in order to overcome the dependence upon expatriates (primarily British, American, and Indian) to teach in secondary schools. In discussing the necessity of providing genuine equality of educational opportunity and a system that provides for the social, political, and economic needs of local citizens, F. C. Z. Cammaerts, Chairman of the Department of Education at the University of Nairobi, has written:

> The important and relevant fact about the need for a total change from the British model of education, to a Kenyan, or at any rate East African model, is that this cannot be done by expatriate teachers.

The expatriate teacher has received his own formal schooling, teacher training (in most cases), teaching experience, in another culture. He usually is in

Kenya on a short term contract (e.g. the American Peace Corps and the British Overseas Volunteers), and although he may identify problems and areas of special concern, he rarely is present on the scene long enough to effect real change. These observations are not only relevant to the issue of training local teachers who will perform throughout their careers in the local context, but also to the teacher trainer coming from a different culture attempting to reform the process of teacher training. He, too, has been trained and gained his experience in another culture; he, too, is usually in the host country on a short term contract; he has the added difficulty of frequently attempting to train teachers to work in an environment with which he is, at best, only superficially familiar.

Conditions at Kenyatta College have always added to the complex task of preparing teachers no matter the national origin of the tutor. Facilities are grossly inadequate, funds for improving them appear to be low among government priorities (in fact, when Mr. Kimalel, the Principal, left in 1970, he stated in an interview that one of his major accomplishments during his tenure was improving the water supply), laboratories are below the standard of a number of secondary schools, books are minimal, selection procedures are unsatisfactory, and perhaps most disconcerting from the point of view of the students, the staff is constantly changing. For example, in the Department of English, no tutor saw the third year students off in December of 1971, who was present when they arrived in May of 1968. Teaching practice is a further source of problems. Schools are inadequate or uncooperative. Private schools frequently do not allow students to teach in the manner they have been prepared at the College. Innovation in teaching techniques is generally frowned upon. Morale tends to be low among students and teachers because the profession is becoming less respected by the community; in some respects it is a "second class" occupation. One frequently hears the comment, "If the students were 'smart' they would go into business or on to the 'real' university."

Yet, it is in this context that teachers for the new nation must be trained. Lacking clear Ministry of Education Directives, and with a strange marriage with the University, all the productive energy available to faculty and students must be exploited in the attempt to mold a functioning institution. However, the makeup of the staff of Kenyatta College makes the performing of this difficult task far less successful than it might be.

Table 1 shows the Nationalities of the seventy-five tutors at Kenyatta College in June of 1969.

TABLE 1

Nationalities of Tutors At Kenyatta College, June, 1969

Nationality	Number
Kenya Citizens	10
British Citizens	33
United States Citizens	18
Other (including Canadian, Indian, Pakistani, Dutch, Czech, Irish)	14

Source: Faculty list published by the College for that period.

Of these, less than half had ever taught in a Kenyan secondary school; only fifteen percent had taught in Kenya for over five years; thirty percent had no academic degree (although many had a Diploma in Education); no Kenyan member of staff had a degree.

But statistics do not even begin to reflect the atmosphere of the College where tutors lived and worked. As the Table indicates, the vast majority of staff (fifty-one of seventy-five) were either British or American. Most of the British were working under UK contracts renewable every two years. A few clerics and several wives were on local contracts. Most of the Americans were at Kenyatta College under the auspices of Teacher Education East Africa, an AID program administered by Teachers College, Columbia University; a few were Roman Catholic nuns and brothers. Although all these people lived virtually next door to each other, even sharing semi-detached houses, and worked in the same academic departments, the relationships, as seen in national terms, directly affected the College's development. Let several specific examples serve to establish the nature of the personal conflicts existing between British and American tutors and their families on the compound.

Even before arriving in Kenya and while attending an "orientation" session at Teachers College, Columbia University, prospective tutors received letters from the American contingent at Kenyatta College, those tutors who had been there almost a year, filled with advice related to the problems of living in a developing country, and most specifically one that was "so British". Upon our arrival, we were met by a throng of Americans who immediately (even on the bus from the airport to the hotel) began informing us of the difficulties we could expect from all these English people, from the Head of the College on down. The following day at breakfast our more experienced colleagues regaled themselves with comments about the bizarre nature of the "English" food we were eating and the strange names applied to things like bacon. The rest of the breakfast conversation revolved around the terrible things that went on in the "English" schools our children might be attending and a strong sales pitch for the "American Community School" which would make our children feel more at home. Trivial in themselves, such comments reveal the pervasiveness of the antagonism, the frustration felt at being what they called "thwarted," not appreciated, not recognized, not listened to, by their British colleagues. Their identity as Americans appeared to be constantly threatened. The Americans (especially the dozen who were with TEEA) were a close knit group spending most of their social time together, and they shared their conclusions about the arrogance, aloofness, chauvinism, self-centeredness, staidness, conservatism, of the British staff and their wives. Attending a large party given by a member of the American contingent a week after our arrival, one could not help but be struck not only by the lack of Africans, but also the complete lack of British accents.

During the first faculty meeting of the year, it became apparent that the proper distribution of mail to faculty was the major issue for consideration. Immediately, it became a national issue. The British were generally satisfied with the rather informal open box dispersal system; the head of the American group, however, informed the session that in his country mail was a "sacred commodity and the privacy of the individual was considered paramount" furthermore, Time magazines (a very obvious American publication) were frequently missing from Americans' mail boxes. He concluded his speech with the comment that, "The British may not care about such matters, but you can be assured that we do." Such observations are anything but conducive to harmony. A related comment was made by an Englishman, with his own arbitrary anti-Americanism which will be discussed later, when he said that the first thing a new American science instructor informed him (perhaps ironically at his mailbox) was that "he had come over to clean up the mess that the British had made." The suspicion was, of course, mutual. This same Englishman, after making a careful point of limiting our conversations to a duration of one sentence during the first four months of our acquaintance invited my family to a pre-Christmas party where he and his paranoic Shropshire pal spent the evening describing all the American products which were in fact made by British companies, extolling the British colonial tradition, and telling my children in confidential tones how fortunate they were to be away from Chicago gangsters, race riots, and a philistine culture and were now allowed to wear uniforms to school. At our departure, they both commiserated with me about the unfortunate circumstances of my choice of birthplace. I was informed by another Englishman that the problem with the Americans was that they were arrogant, exclusive, constantly waving the American flag, provincial, inflexible, and anti-British.

One final anecdote may serve to suggest the effect of such conflicts in relation to the functioning of departments. An American Black, a former University Varsity football player and weight lifter, arrived on the compound to join the Physical Education Department. A member of that Department was a wiry, intense, soccer and cricket playing Englishman, about eighty pounds lighter than the new member. Both were intensely nationalistic, or, perhaps more precisely, highly defensive regarding criticisms of their respective cultures. Not surprisingly, their first meeting in the departmental office led to an increasingly volatile discussion of the relative merits of American and British sports and their place in Kenya. Since the two adversaries shared few sports, but both needed to prove their superiority (and by implication that of their nations) a compromise contest was immediately arranged — in badminton. According to those present, members of both "communities" attended the confrontation. After a grueling two hour match the Englishman, who obviously had the better of the compromise, won. Whereupon, again according to reliable witnesses, the American literally walked through the net breaking his racket into splinters and continued on across the compound to his home (located directly across the street from his opponent) where he was later seen in his back garden furiously lifting huge weights. The next morning, while the Englishman was attempting to fix something under his ancient but very British Anglia sedan, he emerged only to find the American observing his efforts with a bemused smile. Without comment, the American lifted the front of the Anglia motioning for the badminton expert to complete his work. He then held it a foot off the ground for several anxious moments while his visibly nervous but silent neighbor appeared to complete his work. After an abbreviated "thanks" the two separated to continue their new equalized association for two uncomfortable years.

Similar examples, if not quite so dramatic, could be cited. The point is, however, that this atmosphere of mutual suspicion and antagonism permeated the compound. Much of the problem has to do with the nature of expatriate existence. People find themselves removed from familiar surroundings and an atmosphere where expectancies are clearly defined. Now they are suddenly confronted by unprecedented situations, even living styles. As has been suggested, few had experience working with Kenyan students either in a training college or secondary school. Curricula and syllabuses are usually ill-defined which adds to the insecurity of the teachers. Most significantly, the standard of living afforded by the expatriate existence in an underdeveloped country was new to most tutors, British or American. Coming from cultures where the existence of the teacher is anything but "soft", they find themselves with servants who perform all kinds of tasks from serving morning tea, to washing clothes and picking up the garden; they have more money and, by implication, higher prestige than ever before in their lives, and too, a great deal more leisure time. The combination resulted in many members of the faculty and their families becoming rather impressed with their new life styles and themselves, and they rushed about in efforts to prove that they were "to the manor born." One could observe Yorkshiremen with working class backgrounds practicing voice modulations that would suggest a strictly Oxbridge upbringing or Americans who enjoyed sitting over coffee and sharing their "servant problems." The efforts were in most cases amusingly abortive, but the time consumed certainly did not contribute to the training of secondary school teachers. Expatriates were indulging in a way of life dependent upon the poorness of the host country and yet their responsibility was to obviate the necessity of their own presence, to fulfill a temporary requirement while nationals were trained to perform their roles. The result, and it is an old story, was the bureaucratic organization perpetuating itself, the staff generally doing all they could to avoid making themselves "expendable."

Interestingly, there were few Africans on the faculty, and although efforts were made to recruit at least several more members, the efforts were frequently unproductive. Several factors contributed to this situation. First, the local pay was low and educated and qualified Africans could find more lucrative appointments. Second, as long as British and American aid programs were willing to provide technical experts, there was little local motivation to find qualified personnel; in fact, in many cases, the expatriate, frequently with advanced degrees, was cheaper. Third, because of the preponderance of "foreigners" on the staff, Africans frequently felt intimidated and even out of place. They had been successfully indoctrinated throughout their educational progression to believe that local schools were inevitably inferior to their colonial counterparts and even if they were educated abroad, they could never fully partake of the alien culture. For example, the Department Chairmen Meetings, held bi-weekly, included some fourteen members, two of whom were Kenyan. Ironically, the British and Americans carried on debates, usually on national lines, about the best ways to train teachers for Kenya's needs. In seven meetings during the third term of 1969, one Kenyan department head never spoke on any issue. The other twice offered comments but only in relation to teaching practice problems. This lack of African leadership contributed to the vacuum that existed at the College and the lack of connection with the real world of Kenyan secondary school conditions and requirements.

Let us now consider briefly a manifestation of this national conflict with regard to actual curriculum matters at the College. During 1966 and 1967, Americans were responsible for the Education Department of the College and they attempted, with the help of other Americans on the staff, to establish a version of an "American" theoretical model wherein the Education Department was the center of the institution and much emphasis was placed on learning theory, developmental psychology, and innovative teaching methods (individualized instruction, small group work, increased exploitation of multi-media possibilities, the integration of teaching methods and the students' academic learning). However, there was, especially among the British staff, much criticism of the nature of what was being introduced, as well as the manner in which it was being implemented. It was argued that "Those Americans" were attempting to superimpose a model onto the College that ignored accepted practices and local needs. They concluded that attempts were being made to force them to make drastic changes without a clear rationale, that the Education Department was attempting to move too fast, too indiscriminantly. When these Americans left in 1968 (a common theme of the expatriate syndrome alluded to earlier), the Education Department, after floundering for a while due to lack of leadership, was restructured to conform to a more traditional British model by the new Chairman, a science teacher from England with no previous teacher college experience, and his increasingly Kenyanized department. The British staff tended to accept the 1969-70 changes, but many Americans were critical, primarily because they saw the Education Department as too removed from its basic functions in the preparation of teachers — and because they took the changes as an affront. The new Chairman made every effort to seek out opinion from all factions as to the proper role of his Department and found little in the way of consensus. Both sides tended to agree upon reservations far more readily than potential reforms. Evidence suggests that positions were taken after highly subjective rather than pedagogical consideration. Actually, when the Department finally attempted to increase its influence, nationality was not the only issue in the universal reservations expressed by the staff. However, one could see the Americans tending to oppose it because the idea was "British" (two years before it had been identified as "American") and the British saw the whole issue as a compromise to the Americans.

The picture is not entirely bleak, however. Individuals occasionally acted as such, transcending the armed camp atmosphere; barriers could be broken down. Even departments were able to overcome initial prejudices and perform effectively, Table 2 describes the makeup of a particular department, one that was able to create over a two year period an entirely new three and four year syllabus.

TABLE 2

English Department Staff, Kenyatta College, May, 1970

1. Nationality

United States	4
Great Britain	4
India	1

2. Training

    a. One tutor had done formal course work in Teaching English as a Second Language

    b. One tutor had previous experience in the College level

    c. Two tutors did undergraduate major in field other than English

    · d. Three tutors had advanced degrees

    e. Four had experience teaching in a Kenyan secondary school

    f. Two had teacher training experience before coming to Kenyatta College

3. Duration of Employment in Kenya and at Kenyatta College

    a. One tutor had been at the College more than two years (left during term)

    b. Two tutors had worked as teachers in Kenya more than four years

    c. Three tutors terminated contract by end of calendar year

Source: College data on teaching staff and interviews

There had been one Kenya citizen tutor in the English Department in the history of the College (as of 1971) and that tutor had stayed less than a year. Attitudes towards the purposes of education, the role of the teacher training college, the appropriate form a syllabus of English should take, all varied.

However, partially the result of the extensive involvement of former students in the process of change and the constant close association demanded of members of the department as a result of the groups' fortuitous (and that is as scientific as one can become here) commitment to the development of a new syllabus, the Department did produce; it did accomplish what it set out to. As Table 2 indicates, although individuals had gaps in their competencies and experience, except for the lack of a Kenyan in the Department, at least collectively the members had the variety of background required for the task. The close and constant association dictated by the efforts to collectively create the new syllabus (as well as increased involvement in team teaching, master teaching secondary school classes while students observed, development of language laboratory materials, etc.) resulted in increased social contact, which positively affected working relationships. British and Americans ate, drank, went to films, argued together, even shared in the ownership of horses. These activities contributed to breaking down the sterotypes and defenses that we have been considering.

The implications of these observations for the selection and training of American personnel to work and teach in developing countries are worth considering. It often appeared that one of the criteria for the selection of American personnel was an assumed parallel between their rural origins in the United States and agricultural economies of the underdeveloped nation where they would be working. Yet, provinciality and a lack of tolerance for disparate points of view are central to the kinds of conflicts that existed at an institution like Kenyatta College, and these qualities frequently accompanied the Americans to their assignments. Many American tutors had a misguided notion of their missionary roles. They expected to be appreciated and admired, and what proved most disillusioning, well liked by everyone with whom they came into contact. They found that Africans frequently did not choose to take advantage of their willingness to serve (a common complaint of American wives). They found themselves living in a culture which was in many respects more British than African, a condition they had not anticipated.

Orientation programs should account for the problems more directly and make efforts to inform the Americans about the complexity of the environment in which they will be working (an added problem existed here in that because of economic considerations the sponsoring University preferred to do its "orienting" on its own campus). Rather than simply focusing in screening applicants on the problems of prejudice against Blacks, observers should consider the ability of the applicant to function in a variety of environments (for example, of the thirty-seven tutors that went to East Africa under the auspices of TEEA in 1968, eighteen had done all their teaching within a 100 mile radius, and a third of those had worked in only one institution).

The ability to work with people of alien or conflicting values should be considered along with an applicant's sense of security and flexibility. Many of the Americans at Kenyatta College became obsessed with what they described as the lack of efficiency. They criticized the slowness with which change was implemented, the embarrassment of attempting to pick up ordered books at Nairobi bookstores only to be thwarted because of the College's unpaid bills; even the projector at the local movie theater had a perverse way of usually malfunctioning. Each of these matters was taken terribly seriously.

So much of the paranoia which Americans (and British) demonstrated on the compound can be attributed to their lack of a sense of who they are, the nature of the task they are attempting to accomplish, and a sense of proportion about their long range contributions. Several Americans, for example, were highly frustrated because they felt they were not sufficiently appreciated by their superiors; that their efforts, because of the dominant British influence, were going unheralded. This need for external approval as a primary source of gratification creates barriers to effective teaching as well as meaningful cooperation with one's colleagues. Many of these conditions could be anticipated. When one is reminded of how extensive and expensive the screening processes are for most American overseas projects, an indifference to these factors so directly affecting the quality of the technical assistance is inexcusable.

Kenyan students tended to like and appreciate their American teachers and tutors. They found them highly conscientious in their preparation, approachable, committed to their work. Sometimes uncomfortable with the informality and looseness of the classroom atmosphere, they wished that Americans were more aware of the examination structure under which they were functioning. Nevertheless, the American presence in Kenya is strongly and unequivocally felt, and the overall reaction is positive. Despite one American's comment upon his departure that the "British get all the credit, we do all the work," American expatriates working in developing nations need not worry so much about their influence (a quality that pervaded the entire American community throughout Kenya). If they could only relax a bit, not fear to involve themselves with fellow workers and people of the host country, have a sense of humor about themselves and their position, focus their attention on liking rather than needing to be liked (the British are no more sensitive or ignorant than Americans); their skills and knowledge will suffice. All those political concerns will take care of themselves, and the young people of these new nations will be the ones to benefit.

Chapter 10

INNOCENCE ABROAD

Dennis L. Buckley

In 1958, my first education experience abroad began when I was twenty-three. I still have the booklet given to me then by the United States Educational Commission in the Federal Republic of Germany (Fulbright Commission). The tattered and yellowed foreword contains the following advice:

> ". . . . you should understand in advance that you will be faced with problems of readjustment which demand patience and tact. We hope that you are not coming to Germany primarily as a crusader for American ideas and institutions, but rather as an ambassador of good will who approaches new situations with an open mind and a tolerant understanding."

By substituting x country for Germany in the above quotation, the American going abroad to teach in an institution of higher education has some sound counsel. If the American lecturer is going to an English speaking country, one of the most pernicious handicaps to adjustment is the failure to realize that things are different. Secondly, it usually takes a period of culture shock to realize that one must adjust. You are not going to change centuries of tradition, no matter how convinced you are of the superiority of the American Way.

One of the first steps toward a successful adjustment to working in a foreign institution of higher education is to become cognizant of the assumptions underlying American education. In other words, to understand the American bias in matters educational. I use the work bias advisedly; a serious student of comparative education soon realizes that value-laden terms such as "good" and "bad" cannot be applied to foreign education *in vitro*. But what are the American biases in education?

R. Freeman Butt spent six months in Australia in 1954. His impressions during this brief span of time are still valuable today. And in addition to pointing up the assumptions underlying Australian education, he clearly outlined his own frame of reference. As often happens, a stay in a foreign country, in a foreign educational institution, makes one more aware of what one's own beliefs about education are. Butt writes in the first chapter of his booklet:

"I assume that in a democratic and complex society education should be available freely and equally to all people. In general I believe in more education for more people rather than a little education for the few. The educational base of a democratic society should be broad and generous. I believe in equality of educational opportunity rather than in a stratified dual system of education whether that dualism be along lines of race, religion, economic status, social class, or sheer intellectual ability.[1]

Since 1955, of course, these beliefs have been shown rather conclusively to be myths, but nonetheless Americans share this belief at the gut level. The fact remains that the American educational system is unique in its attempts at implementing these beliefs.

The conclusions for the American educationist abroad are obvious. He will not be in a democratic educational system; he will find himself within a system more or less influenced by an elitist philosophy of education.[2] And as an associate member he will benefit from the exclusiveness of the foreign academic club. His status (if not his salary) will be higher than it was in the United States. The students, on the other hand, because they are already fledgling members of the elite, are less apt to comply with the demands of academic drudgery than are their counterparts in the States. Crucial selection has already occurred earlier within the system, and the student's social upward mobility has now become sponsored and somewhat removed from contested mobility.[3]

The foreign student will expect and demand scintillating lectures but feel uncomfortable when called upon to discuss ideas. He would rather write them down on paper, and he does a good job at it — generally better than his American counterpart. The foreign student will certainly not buy texts nor is he apt to read prescribed materials as basis for discussion. A good deal of this attitude can be explained by the British "gentleman scholar" concept. Leisure is necessary for true brilliance to express itself. The gentleman's "C" is certainly sufficient — for there are other matters of more seriousness than the petty work of schoolboys. There are exceptions of course, but the above generalizations might well prepare the American academic for a shock.

A word should be said about the machinations of bureaucratic intrigue with one's peers at the particular foreign institution of higher learning.

---

[1] *Assumptions Underlying Australian Education*, first published in 1955 with eight reprints (the last, February, 1970) by the Australian Council for Educational Research, p.4.

[2] It should be noted here that the present writer does not consider a national system of education which gives a particular segment of the society a better education to be inherently bad. However, the degree to which the elite are determined by inherited rather than acquired qualifications is my biased indicator of "bad" system of education.

[3] I use these terms in the sense of Ralph H. Turner's paper, "Sponsored and Content Mobility and the School System." *American Sociological Review*, 1960, pp. 855-867.

Refreshingly, academic gamesmanship is international in its basic motives — the game is the same but with slightly different rules.[4] If you are to lecture at a university, the most important activity is to be writing an article or book, or at least to be able to talk about writing an article or book. Your colleagues abroad will quickly recognize this as a mark of status. On the other hand, if you are lecturing at a teachers' college or small liberal arts college in another country, lip service will be paid to your ability as a teacher. The halo effect of popularity might then be assiduously cultivated to raise your status as teacher.[5] Attendance at a few student parties and even a party of your own for the students will do wonders. The foreign student will appreciate this doubly, since foreign lecturers maintain more social distance from their underlings than do their American counterparts.

The administrators of tertiary education will disappoint the American visitor, for they are not generally trained as administrators. This may come as a surprise to the American academic, for unless he has been abroad before he will probably have concluded that no country could have worse administrators than the United States. Yankee know-how should not be underestimated and its true value will be most appreciated in a foreign setting of organizational chaos and incompetency. The great American academic dream — that the administrative *raison d'etre* is to assist in the task of education — has not been dreamt abroad. More so than in the States, the foreign administrative bloc has been at work long enough to be self-perpetuating and to be too concerned with their own maintenance and proliferation to be bothered with matters of education. Pride in organizational efficiency is uniquely American.

There are compensations for bureaucratic bunglings, however. The American lecturer will find that few people will know what he is really doing, nor will they be overly concerned. The resultant freedom is intoxicating to the visiting academic. Coupled with a lower teaching load, there is every opportunity to explore and to learn from your hosts.

If your stay in the host country is to be short, the remainder of this paper need not be read. However, the job market for Ph.D.'s being what it is in the United States,[6] it might be well to consider serious steps toward becoming accepted by your hosts.

One could list a series of do's and don't's for integration into an English speaking foreign country, but there is also a body of tested methodology

---

[4] See Pierre Van den Berghe, *Academic Gamesmanship*, (Abelard-Schuman, New York, 1970).

[5] Frank Costin and William T. Greenough, "Student Ratings of College Teaching: Reliability, Validity and Usefulness." *Review of Educational Research*, vol. 41, No. 5, p. 517.

[6] And it's not going to get any better. See Allan M. Cartter, *The Journal of Human Resources*, Madison, University of Wisconsin (Summer, 1966), 1, No. 1, cited in Philip H. Coombs, *The World Educational Crisis*, (Oxford Press, New York, 1968), pp. 36-37.

which I have found to be quite helpful.[7] The methodology of participant-observation lends itself well for the visitor who wants to adjust rather than irritate.

The American lecturer abroad is by definition a quasi-participant in the vast dimension of the term. He will remain an outsider in the affective dimension by reason of his pronounciation of the Queen's English. The set of values which were discussed earlier in this paper will provide further reasons for him being labeled as an outsider — especially if the American is vociferous in his espousal of these values. By toning down the more flagrant Americanisms in his speech and by assuming a cultural relationist's position in matters of educational values, he is more apt to become a genuine participant. In a foreign setting, hypocritical humility is of more value than honest arrogance.

The point is that there is so much to learn about the foreign culture and academic subculture that one can ill afford to discourage free intercouse with the informants. To this end the American novitiate should devote a major portion of his time to mastering social situations. Faithful attendance at morning and afternoon teas for the staff is essential to acquiring a knowledge of the personal and institutional values of one's colleagues. Participation in staff parties in order to observe the host country's party etiquette (and avoid a few unnecessary *faux pas*) is a prerequisite to staging your own parties. Nor should you expect your guests automatically to become enamored of the Great American Cocktail.

At the beginning of his experience the American guest should be extremely careful of becoming identified with one particular clique of staff. Cues for identifying the most powerful clique in the academic structure are apt to be different or more subtle than they are on the American scene. It is not meant that the American become a social chameleon; rather he should be careful in joining a particular clique's denunciation of members of another clique. The best excuse is ignorance, and the American abroad has a degree of *Narrenfreiheit* (fool's freedom) which will be tolerated — at least initially.

In addition to the methodology of participant-observation, the foreign environment factor can well be dealt with in the category of field studies. Daniel Katz gives an excellent review of the literature, and also provides an illuminating body of down-to-earth advice.[8] Although the American lecturer may not be primarily concerned with researching his hosts, the following outline provides a guide for things to look for in order to understand your host institution:

---

[7] See, for example, the appropriate sections in Claire Seltiz, Marie Jahoda, Morton Dentsch, and Stuart W. Cook, *Research Methods in Social Relations* (Holt, Rinehart, and Winston, New York, 1965). For a specific discussion of this type of research applied to a foreign setting, see my (as yet) unpublished Ph.D. dissertation, "The German Gymnasium in Flux: A Case Study", UCLA, 1971.

[8] "Field Studies", chapter two, in Leon Festinger and Daniel Katz, eds., *Research Methods in the Behavioral Sciences*, (Dryden Press, New York, 1953).

1. A description of the total structure under study with respect to the major groups and subgroupings.

2. The central value systems and goals of the total system and its various groups.

3. The nature and types of conflicts and points of tension both with respect to the total structure and with respect to a single group.

4. The formal and informal structure and the way in which they are interrelated.

5. The accepted pathways to group goals, including

    a. the logical relation between paths and goals

    b. the remoteness of paths from ultimate goals, or the number of subgoals between a group's activity and its ultimate goal.

    c. the degree of fixation upon one or two main paths, and the range of permissible alternate routes.

6. The degree of autonomy of functioning of the parts within the total structure and the nature of their dependency upon one another and upon the larger whole.

7. The nature of the dependency of the structure under study on the society or larger unit of which it is a part.

8. The power or influence patterns within the structure and its subgroups.

9. The nature of the group sanctions and the degree and basis of their acceptance by group members.

10. The patterns and channels of communication within the structure and the substructures.[9]

In addition to adjusting to one's host institution after having acquired an understanding of it, the American lecturer abroad will have to come to terms with the host culture in general. One of the first reactions of the American abroad is to notice the lack of certain cultural accouterments uniquely

[9] *Ibid.* p. 68.

American. His second reaction is to gripe about the gap in his baggage of accustomed leisure pursuits. The all-American male will certainly bemoan the absence of his favorite televised football and basketball games. Ms. America will miss the variety of programs unique to American television. Cheer up! The gaps can be filled quite adequately with the leisure pursuits of the host culture. Besides, there are generally compensations for the lack of things American. Take television, for example. Although there is a limited range of programs to watch, the quality of the programs is appealing to a better-educated viewer. The exhileration of being able to watch a program on national television without being insulted with commercials for twelve minutes of the viewing hour will more than make up for the limited offerings.

The younger male lecturer abroad will have the opportunity to develop an interest in local sports by playing on an amateur team of cricket (skills similar to baseball), or if he is still physically fit, rugby and soccer. In addition he will have ample opportunity to play or be a spectator at the international sports, e.g., golf and tennis. Incidentally, baseball and basketball are acquiring international status, so the possibility of participating in these sports has increased.

Rest assured, the international pastime of social drinking is pursued avidly in your host country and may well provide an opportunity for excellence in performance for the American. On the other hand, if you are addicted to the virtues of the dry martini, you are in for a disappointment. The solution, of course, is to make your own or to instruct a patient bartender. But one should not overlook the qualities of the host country's national drink. Taste is acquired, and the social settings for acquiring this taste are varied and entertaining.

Having thus disposed of the two most important American leisure activities, television and drinking, only a brief word need be said about other extra-curricular activities. The classical expressions of culture will be found in greater and cheaper abundance than in the States. Plays, ballet, opera, films, museums are readily accessible to their devotees. American products in the form of films, rock musicals, and theatre are also flooding the foreign market.

The absence of the amenities of western technological society which have come to be labeled necessities by Americans may result in a nagging series of frustrations, but they too can be dealt with. No telephone at home or the expense and delays in obtaining one are factors compensated for by the absence of the incessant janglings of that instrument of public intrusion upon one's privacy. Another beneficial side effect is the resulting necessity to plan your social activities in advance with the built-in guarantee that your own social sphere will not be unexpectedly invaded as often as it is in the United States. In your host country, you may find it easier not to own an automobile, because the system of public transportation is more adequate and costs of purchasing and maintaining a car are proportionately higher to one's income than is the case in the States. If one chooses to crawl out from under the thumb of General Motors, the new financial freedom is intoxicating. You will actually be better able to explore your host country geographically and culturally.

To summarize, it is hoped that the American who is going abroad to lecture in a tertiary institution of education in an English speaking country will recognize and accept the following points:

1. Although the language may be basically the same, the culture and institutions are different.

2. Make a concentrated effort to understand the differences.

3. Accept the differences and adjust to them.

To make your stay in another country enjoyable remember that the difference between an inconvenience and an adventure is merely a frame of mind.

Chapter 11

THE AMERICAN PRESENCE IN MIDDLE EAST
HIGHER EDUCATION

Blaise Donadio

The uniqueness of Americans working in Middle East institutions of higher education is characterized by the initial and lasting impression on both the Americans and the Arabic people — expectations are greater than realizations. The complex elements of the hoped-for versus the actual can be focused upon by analyzing the discrepancies between a passive position and active participation. I will attempt to examine some of these discrepancies, as a result of my visits to universities in the Middle East to review programs in English as a Second Language, and from reports and case studies in which I was either involved directly or which were brought to my attention.

A rapidly increasing number of Americans have recently become interested in teaching opportunities abroad, many of them in the developing countries of the Middle East. Numerous educational institutions in this region are in desperate need of competent and understanding foreign educators to complement their academic programs. To the American such opportunity provides an ideal setting for dedicated teaching where it can benefit a willing and developing society. On the other hand, Middle Eastern educators look to the American for quick and easy answers to any and all problems in education, especially those who are studying in English. Consequently, disappointments on both sides are often immediate as well as continuous. There is an overabundance of disparities in communicating which are not at all conducive to mutual understanding.

The great expectations of Middle Easterners concerning Americans began long before there were institutions for higher learning. Generally, to them there has always been the aura, the mystique, and the charisma to that labeled "American," which must be seen and heard to be believed. This influential impression is still glaringly evident today in the preference of so many Middle Eastern people for American music, television, movies, literature, dress styles and automobiles. These are all means to the almost perfect way of life. This informal, inarticulate, ideological concept of the American "thing" is, paradoxically, both an inspiration and an encumbrance. For example, if you were to ask almost any secondary or college student in the Middle East who the American actor, David Janssen, was, the immediate knowing reply would be: "He's the fugitive." Oddly, an American drama teacher in the Middle East miserably failed in producing a school play based on *The Fugitive* television feature. Why? The young people are still bound in their own conventions and customs. Had the teacher let the students write their own script on a similar theme, the language and action of the play might have had more meaning to them. The concepts would have been reinterpreted for the mutual benefit of actors and audience alike.

A vital issue facing American educators in foreign lands is that learning in a second language cannot be equitably approached and evaluated in the same manner as first language concepts and competencies. If their expectations of competence are unrealistic, serious disappointments result for students who may never attain mastery of the English language because they have no familiar landmarks or guidelines.

Prior to the 1940's, virtually all the educational institutions in the Middle East were operated by foreigners, largely American foreigners. Most were missionary and church-society schools. There were also government schools in the protectorates which were subject to the benevolences of the Governors and sometimes unscrupulous native officials. In the few countries attaining self-direction, their economies could not support more than a minimal few years of rudimentary learning. The post-war years brought with them nationalization and free education for all Middle Eastern children. There was aid from American Foundations, the United Nations and the U.S. Peace Corps. There was great expansion in private schools. The list of benevolent agencies helping schools and universities in the Middle East is large and impressive. Among helpful organizations, especially those involved in oil, were included: the Ford Foundation, the Rockefeller Foundation, the General Service Foundation, Near East Emergency Donations, the Crenshaw Corporation, Forest Funds, the Wallace Fund, the Standard Oil (Indiana) Foundation, the Arabian American Oil Company, the American Independent Oil Company, the California Texas Oil Company, the Mobil Oil Corporation, International Business Machines, the Singer Company, and Trans World Airlines. Those who pioneered the development of English language education in the Middle Eastern schools influenced the emergence of universities which reflected American education principles and practices. Despite difficulties in diplomatic relations between the U.S. and Middle Eastern countries, academic relations and cultural exchanges have continued to grow and prosper.

With the decades of British occupation and expanding American enterprises, the English language has become the language of commerce in the Middle East. English is currently taught as *the* second language in all the schools of the Middle East. However, though many students are recruited by colleges and universities with English programs, only a few of these students ever acquire the conceptualization skills and vagaries of the idiom which lead to first-language competency.

Outstanding and unique Americans have also made profound and lasting effects on Middle Easterners. An example of such influence has been the life and work of the eminent American judge, Jasper Brinton, who became the first President of the International Court in Egypt some fifty years ago. Currently in his early nineties, he is still revered as the Dean of International Jurists. His Cairo home is the scene of frequent visits by distinguished diplomats, lawyers, authors, and educators. After "tea with the Brintons" you can recognize the experience of the rare personification of the "mystique Americana." This majestic simplicity and warmth of Americans dedicated to service in foreign lands is unrelated to political or economic postures. It comes under the heading of friendship. Another American byword in her own lifetime is Martha Roy, now seventy years of age, who is still tirelessly teaching Middle Eastern young people in English, French, and Arabic. There are other examples of notables in other fields of endeavor such as the phenomenal achievements of Pere Ayrout among the peasants, and the staff of U.S. Navy Medical Research Units in tropical disease control.

With history on their side, why are some teachers who venture into Middle Eastern educational institutions from the United States usually disappointed in their contributions to educational development? Is it administration of the programs? Culture shock? Academic standards? Financial problems? Communication? Conveniences? Faculty rapport? Students? Social activities? Professional growth difficiences? My observations and study over a two-year period suggests that teachers were confronted with most of these questions in varying amounts of compensatory satisfaction.

One example of the issues faced concerns a teacher who taught a Freshman Humanities Program on a Middle Eastern College campus situated in the very heart of a city just off the busiest downtown street to students who had several years of English language study. The campus itself was complemented by the cacophonous bustle of conglomerate traffic, a contrastingly cool oasis of calm greenery, and an unhurried academic tranquility. Behind its crenelated arabesque walls were fresh green lawns, tennis courts, ornate benches, and arbored walkways reminiscent of American ivy league colleges. A relatively little known institution outside the Middle East, the college was an extremely influential institution, which for the past half-century had weathered wars, revolutions, and strained diplomatic relations. Somewhat old-fashioned by today's American multiversity standards, it provided a heady educational brew for Middle Eastern students. They found the school extremely exciting, especially after attending traditional lower schools where they were spoonfed information which they would parrot back to satisfy the requisites for acquisition of knowledge.

The teacher in question soon learned what critical handicaps all of these influences were to students who were expected to achieve first-language ability through their traditional education methods and her own teaching preferences. How could they summarize required knowledge without reference to texts? How could they compare and contrast related topics in written and oral assignments? How could they prepare a final term paper relevant to the theme of the semester project? How could anyone possibly hear above the noise outside? Besides, these students were accustomed only to rote learning.

The teacher, in addressing the existent problems, designed her course in a number of exciting ways. She devised all sorts of interesting translation exercises; she incorporated a variety of reading and discussion projects; she provided numerous writing alternatives about subjects which were intriguing to students; and she gave great latitude in the development of term papers. She did all she could to help her students.

Yet, despite her positive efforts, she could not in good conscience give any of her students a passing grade at the end of the third semester of the English Humanities Program.

Why? Isn't it the teacher's fault if students don't pass? Perhaps the standards were to high? There were many reasons that the students were unsuccessful, even under the guidance of a superior teacher. Some of them were historical; some, circumstantial. Many of the students were not even proficient in their own language of Arabic, much less English. All had learned English grammar and literature in separate course dosages. Everyone of them had successfully advanced to the Humanities program through a pass-fail examination system.

Ultimately, after much haranguing and discourse, all students were granted a "conditional pass" in the program by a Special Sequestrator (Ombudsman with the authority to act).

The well-intended and hardworking teacher, only desiring to better the system and provide a quality education to her students, did not accept the contract proffered to her for the following year. She believed in adhering to realistic standards, not going through windmill-like motions.

Historically, according the *Encyclopedia of Educational Research,* The teaching of English has lagged more than twenty-five years behind leading scholarship and research in other fields. Language and literature have been all too innocently isolated from one another. The conventions of identifying "English" with "grammar," apart from literature still does prevail in the United States with widespread exception. However, this separation is adhered to unequivocally in the teaching of English as a Second Language overseas. Only very limited use is made of modern techniques in linguistics, transformational grammar, and other new approaches to language study. The phenomenally successful methods of the Army Language School, Monterrey, California, in the teaching of English as a first or second language have gone unnoticed by many professionals. After little more than one year at the Army Language School, graduates' successes are met with such reactions as:

"I don't care if he doesn't like borscht, he's as Russian as I am."

"Yes. He sounds just like my uncle from Hankow."

"He speaks, reads, and writes both classical and colloquial Arabic as well as any graduate of the Al-Azhar."

And as regards the foreigner learning English, the same reactions are noted:

"One year and he sounds like he's straight out of Kansas City."

"He's as American as I am."

Achievement in the languages of the Western world are even more remarkable and are not credited to endless months of study with grammarians.

In the Middle East, English has now replaced French as the second language. Unfortunately, it may be many years before English materials and methods will be available for elementary and secondary schools, and universities. The most critical need is still the proper training of native teachers in their knowledge and use of English and in their application of modern teaching principles. Consequently, students in the Middle East who attend secondary schools to study in English have a pronounced advantage in meeting the language admissions requirement for study in English in an institution of higher learning. Graduates of the native secondary schools which do not have programs in English invariably have to take preparatory studies in English through the British Council facilities or an English Language Institute. Most seem to prefer to study in a language institute administered by Americans. No matter the preparatory program, grave difficulties are still ahead of students because a single, composition-type of final examination in English determines proficiency. The fatalities of the examination are often as high as 85% of the applicants for admission and 50% of the first semester freshmen.

However, most of the applicants pass the grammar part of the admissions test. Most fail in composition. The emphasis on grammar does not provide the language familiarity needed for reading with comprehension, recognition, and use of proper idiom. It does not allow for conceptualization, analytical comparison and contrast. It does not encourage creative writing, thesis writing, and translation effectiveness. Words, rather than meaning are learned; vowels and consonants, rather than concepts.

What is being done to alleviate some of these problems? There have been recent reappraisals of curricula. There has been much interest in new educational innovations in the recruitment of talented teachers. At one university where less than half the faculty are Americans, special instruction and exposition in Arabic had become increasingly necessary to enable students to cope with the difficulties of advanced study. In one instance, several departments had to prevail upon members of the English Department to reorganize its Freshman Program. This was seen as a fundamental step toward more competent performances in English in all fields: comparative analytical study; comprehending and synthesizing knowledge being acquired in each course; pursuing knowledge in addition to or independent of course requirements; and involvement in class discussions and presentations where critical and creative thinking was essential to reading, lecture materials, and class discussion.

There are inherent difficulties and limitations, as well as great expectations, in teaching at the Middle Eastern university level where English is the second or third language for the students. A critical problem is the reluctance of the student to admit that he does not understand an explanation, a reading assignment, a lecture, or a topic for discussion or composition. This recognition is a realistically basic premise for principles underlying the philosophy and psychology of studying in English as a Second Language in the Middle East. Open the catalog of one of the universities and you will find a statement of purpose much like the following:

> Our goals are to offer liberal American education to students of the Middle East and foster understanding of the Arab World in the West. In research, the University undertakes and encourages others to undertake, studies which benefit the Arab world by advancing the sciences of today and rediscovering the arts of the past. In both teaching and research, the University emphasizes programs and approaches which complement the activities of the National Institutions.

The gap between stated goals and the implementation of such goals can most effectively be bridged through viable principles of teaching and learning in a second language. These principles should be practiced in daily in-class programs and out-of-class activities. It is depressing to hear American teachers of English say: "Let's face it, these kids are not college material" or "These students can't think for themselves, they have to memorize everything." These are the same teachers who present grammar, reading, and composition so that good memorization makes it simple to pass their tests. This is not learning; it is not application.

One of the difficulties in evaluating English as a Second Language program is obtaining honest evaluation on the part of students. Historically, people of the Middle East have been characteristically highly respectful of their teachers under even the most adverse circumstances. In spite of the growing acceptance of Western ideas, this Occidental influence on education, together with dependence upon rote learning, has changed little. I know of an American psychology professor, in a Middle Eastern University, single and an avid traveler, who met with his classes little more than half the time. He gave extensive research assignments and difficult tests, but he never returned any papers to his students. At the end of the term, he failed or gave "incompletes" to the majority of his students. All of them accepted their unfair fate without question, holding the Professor in high esteem. It was only when they were interrogated in confidence, as a result of an investigation by a Special Sequestrator, in Arabic, that the students expressed their anxieties about the course and the matter could be given proper resolution.

Expedience is no substitute for the proper implementation of declared goals; nor can assumptions be made that all is well in the absence of complaint. The reluctance to make commitments to resolve difficulties can all be summed up in the paramount issue of communication. There are many fine, successful programs where good communications are evident, but it appears that non-communication situations are the rule rather than the exception. Dedicated teaching is a vital factor toward willingness to promote the fullness of communication in a second language program in the Middle East. We cannot overlook the highly significant cultural role of communication evidenced through the "American presence." The thoughts and actions of Middle Eastern people have been affected in ways beyond the educational, and political context. In the words of the late Bayard Dodge, President of the American University in Beirut from 1913 to 1948, "The important thing is trying to maintain American goodwill and prestige. They've found that the University does more than anything else to keep up goodwill for the people of the country towards America. It's a counter-irritant to some of the things the Arabs don't like. The Arabs don't like the U.S. Government policy, but they really do like Americans."[1]

I think that those words are still quite true.

---

[1] "A Talk with Bayard Dodge", by Elizabeth and John R. Starkey in *Aramco World*, bi-monthly magazine published by the American Arabian Oil Company, by Paul F. Hoye, 505 Park Avenue, New York, New York 10022, July-August, 1972.

Chapter 12

THE INTERNATIONAL
SCHOOL PRINCIPAL

Albert A. Chudler

School closed because of political riots, termites invading the bookroom, wild animals and reptiles roaming around buildings, teachers just arriving from the States not permitted to enter the country because of visa problems, students arrested for drugs, thirty different nationalities represented in the school, the budget reduced unexpectedly by the dollar devaluation — such are the realities with which the overseas principal must deal. And they represent only a random sample of the many challenges and experiences an international school principal will face. In the beginning you think such problems are insurmountable; as time goes on, you learn to contend with them.

Are there specialized courses of training which can prepare an administrator to serve in a foreign setting to anticipate and effectively meet the many challenges? I doubt it very much. Overseas service in education requires an individual who is world-minded, a person who is able to identify with the peoples of other countries and cultures. The varied facets of leadership demanded by a typical international school cannot be taught; they must be learned experientially.

Vision, human relations skills, initiative, and common sense are all helpful. A deep concern for the well-being of humanity is another prerequisite for the principal. All aspects of school administration are his responsibility: curriculum, supervision of staff, discipline, plant management, guidance, personnel, public relations, and finance. He makes the final decisions. The buck stops at his desk. Respect of the staff, student body, community, and board members must also be maintained or he may as well pack up and go home. But that respect must be earned.

An American school in a foreign setting is constantly on exhibit. Your ability to work with all kinds of people is of prime importance. Quite often, the custodial and secretarial staff members are local nationals. They are the community lookouts who can observe whether you are attempting to sincerely comprehend their culture and society or you are just another American bureaucrat. Local educators will want to see what you have to offer that is different. Thus, sincere humility must be displayed. This interest on the part of professionals in the country in which you are a guest provides opportunities to exchange and share educational ideas and philosophies. Such interchange should not be comparisons of which systems are better, but what each educational concept or method has to offer to the other culture.

Even if you can interact with foreign educators, you often feel educationally isolated. You feel remote from the mainstream of the educational excitement and change which you hadn't realized had provided you with such invisible motivation. Developmental and in-service educational opportunities in most foreign countries are practically non-existent. You must be professionally self-propelled.

Bring along your own professional library, your files. You will be grateful you have them. There is usually a dearth of such materials in your new overseas setting. Maintain subscriptions to professional magazines. Share them with your staff. You have to take charge of in-service training. Don't forget to hound educational publishers. Those brochures and sales promotions they send do keep one abreast of new curriculum materials and educational activity. Explore correspondence courses which would be of interest to you and your staff. Stay in close touch with your professional colleagues back home as to new developments and ideas. Find out who may be traveling through your area who could speak or work with your staff and students. Bringing different resource people to your school can also provide objective evaluations of what is being accomplished or neglected.

Before assuming an overseas assignment, saturate yourself with information about the culture you will be entering. Consult your predecessor to learn as much as possible about the local school, staff personalities, major problems and issues, and the community. Explore your school or public library for materials and books about the country in which you will be working. There is so much to absorb. A good headstart will enhance your possibilities for a successful assignment.

Prepare your family, as well. The more knowledgeable they are about the customs and traditions of a country, the more apt everyone is to avoid severe cultural shock. Many an overseas school administrator has gone under because either he or his family have been culturally unprepared. Seemingly small idiosyncracies become significantly important when you are overseas, both on your part and the host nationals'. For example, in Asia the beckoning gesture of the hand indicating "Please come here" is palm down. In western cultures, it is palm up. If an Asian policeman was frantically signaling for your presence and you were just as frantically running in the opposite direction, a number of difficulties might ensue. If one learns the proper way to do things too late, he can make poor impressions which will be difficult to live down. Unfortunately, those first impressions are often the most indelible ones.

Once you arrive on the job, you will be expected to produce immediately. There is little or no orientation, no pre-service training, just total immersion. Staff, community, and board members will all look to you for instant and demonstrative leadership. From the very beginning, you must exude confidence, display intelligence, and make decisions without offending anyone. This is terribly difficult, particularly when you don't even know the cast of characters in the drama you have entered. Too often, staff members who have been attached to an overseas school for a long time are the most threatened by a new administrator, and the most defensive. One of your difficult tasks is developing a trust with everyone with whom you come in contact. To a great extent, this is how your eventual success will be determined.

Enriching the current and developing the new curriculum should also be among your prime tasks. Generally, the programs in overseas schools are academically-oriented, since a large proportion of students are college-bound. It is virtually impossible for anyone to be a specialist in all learning areas. Nevertheless, it is essential that the overseas administrator be able to understand the scope and sequences of each grade and subject area. He has the major responsibility to direct the staff in visualizing the overall curriculum planning picture and to encourage the sharing of staff skills and talents.

In most overseas instances, teacher turnover is high. A hodge-podge curriculum can exist when the backgrounds of the teachers differ. They usually control what takes place in their own classrooms. Thus, there must be mutual discovery of ways to develop an inclusive sequential curriculum which will meet the various needs of students. This requires informed, stimulated, and responsible leadership. Enlist the full support of staff in all of these endeavors. It is their involvement which will ensure success. They have too much at stake themselves not to be an integral part of the academic decision-making process.

Naturally, each overseas school is unique in terms of faculty, building facilities, and local regulations. Fortunately, the overseas American administrator usually has a great deal of freedom in planning the school programs. A caution! As you and your faculty institute curriculum innovations, keep the board members, parents, and students informed about such changes. Anticipate them, so that you can have understanding in the beginning, rather than confusion at the point of implementation.

By all means, know the strengths and weaknesses of your faculty. In a small overseas school, you and members of your staff will be called upon to perform activities or speak to groups in areas in which you lack experience or preparation. This could range from explaining the U.S. foreign policy as it pertains to overseas oil exploration to a government official's indiscretion with a local resident. Additionally, personal sacrifices must be made for the benefit of students. You miss your vacation to chaperone them on theirs. You continuously open your home to students whose parents are away on business or pleasure. Be realistic about your own capabilities, especially your tolerance levels.

In an American school overseas, it is necessary that significant emphasis be placed on the development of intercultural appreciation. The local language, the history and geography, and the customs and traditions of the host country should be taught to all children at all levels. With a minimum of encouragement and preparation you and your students spend an inspirational week on a Japanese farm or a Malaysian rubber plantation. You have much more freedom in planning such excursions overseas than in the States. What better way can children learn about people than to be with or to live with them? Of course, there are precautions which must be taken. Iodine tablets may be needed to purify the water. Netting may be required for protection from the many insects in some areas. Certain essential foods may have to be transported which are unavailable where you are going.

If many nationalities are represented in a school, the curriculum should reflect this international component of education. Having a multi-cultural student body greatly strengthens a curriculum. It enables understanding and respect for each individual to exist. Human dignity is all important. Parents can also help in this area. They can speak to classes, share slides, embassy films, and artifacts. They can assist as classroom volunteers. Overseas, parents have an uncommon opportunity to contribute to and participate in the total school program. A wise principal can expand his total human resources greatly in adding and absorbing a parent cadre.

Occasionally, local national teacher organizations are anxious for contacts with American teachers. Some conferences on education are sponsored to which your teachers are invited. Encourage them to take every advantage to meet with foreign teachers. By participating with host country educators, your teachers are able to increase their knowledge of the country and quickly expand their backgrounds. They, too, have to have opportunities to make the curriculum exciting, to make it meaningful, and to make it constructive.

Problems which principals have which are related to salary and other compensations for faculty can be extremely complex. There are shifting exchange rates; salary considerations for Americans hired locally, in the States, or local nationals. Salary credits must be established for different kinds of training and credentials, for varying lengths of service. Proper housing for staff members can cause all kinds of awkward situations. Inequities are inevitable. But where real or apparent inequities exist, the explanations should be clear and honest. The lines of communication must remain open. Difficult as it may be at times, the welfare of pupils must be placed before the personal concerns of staff.

Finding teaching substitutes is another frustration for the overseas principal. It is not unusual to be faced with the sudden resignation of a teacher in the middle of a school year. A teacher's husband has been suddenly transferred. The death of a relative causes a teacher's Stateside return. A staff member becomes ill. As an overseas school principal, you must be much more aware of all the human resources in the community than in the States. You have to be crisis-oriented.

Orientation programs for new teachers, not only to the school, but the community, are most vital. These programs should be planned for teachers and their families. A lonely wife in a foreign country can completely demoralize a teacher. In considering entire families in planning such programs, you soon learn that the individual family units can become a most wonderful school family with friendships developed which future years only strengthen. I have so many fond memories of the warmth and unity of our school community that it is hard to recall all of them.

An overseas community is usually an intricate one. It involves families that come from all over the world, as well as the local national community in which the school is geographically and culturally located. Generally, as the chief administrator of the school, you will be invited to functions sponsored by the host country, as well as the diplomatic missions in the area. You are the chief representative for the school in all community activities. In such a role, you will have ample opportunity to display your personal educational wares. You may also be the only resident American.

Constant contact with the host country government, especially the red tape which always rears its recurring head in dealing with government bureaucracies, can be demanding. Patience and a sensitivity to the "working mind" of the people of the country is required. Be especially alert to developing cooperative working relationships with officials of local government agencies. They can assist you immensely in emergencies.

Discover whether or not enrollment of the local children of the foreign country is encouraged or discouraged. If this is not considered, you can find yourself in all kinds of difficulty. Also, the hiring of host country teachers must be seriously considered. On the one hand, this can really improve public relations. On the other, it could mean sacrificing educational quality. Usually, in such areas as art, music, physical education, and foreign language, local teachers can be real assets. They stabilize a school as well as add an international "flavor" to the staff. Always remember, you are advancing a rather evasive U.S. culture in a foreign setting. Your curriculum must be geared to the mechanizations of American articulation.

Be aware of local custom regulations on the import of books and supplies. In some countries, books and filmstrips must be reviewed by government authorities when they arrive in the country. Censorship is not unusual. If you are not aware of the political philosophy of the host country, you're really in trouble. I've seen too many overseas educators waste money on ordering materials that were never received. They're gathering rust or dust in a warehouse accessible only to the security officers of a foreign land.

Book and equipment orders to the States must be submitted months in advance. Even with seemingly ample time, you are never certain materials will arrive in time for the opening of school. If you run short of textbooks, months can elapse before you receive additional copies. If you can afford to be extravagant, you can have them shipped by air. However, I've seen a book handed daily from child to child because it was the only one in algebra or on the American revolution. Thank heaven, many teachers bring many books from their own libraries to their overseas posts.

At times, the problems and frustrations of being an overseas principal may seem overwhelming. Yet, patience and persistence can bring rewards which could never be experienced in any other situation. You have uncommon opportunities to mold and influence an entire international community, knowing that you are helping to educate boys and girls, while emphasizing the international dimensions of education.

Serving as an administrator in an international school in an international setting makes you an international administrator. You will become intimately better acquainted with another society and culture. You will develop a network with educators in other parts of the world. You will grow immensely.

Above all, have a deep respect for your fellow man. You are traversing the earth together, as are your respective countries. You have the responsibility to make an international school a center for world understanding. You can help create an island of hope in a holocaust of confusion.

Chapter 13

EDUCATIONAL TECHNICAL ASSISTANCE
AND LATIN AMERICAN DEPENDENCE

Thomas J. La Belle

Foreign Influence and Educational Dependence in Latin America

As is typical among nations that have experienced colonial status, much of Latin American educational development has been dependent upon patterns which were either imposed or borrowed from outside the region itself. Although formal schooling existed at the time of the conquest among the more complex indigenous societies in Latin America, such institutions were either replaced or substituted for by the carriers of the faith and the seekers of gold from the Iberian peninsula.

As Spain became a leader in teaching and learning during her Golden Age (15th to 17th Century), schools and scholars multiplied and thereby flourished the motivation for the perpetuation of humanism in the Graeco-Roman tradition, the education of an elite, and the spread of Catholicism. In the New World, the prime transmitters of education were the Spanish priests, especially the Jesuits, who were charged with the building of schools, the training of teachers, and the education of the populace for correct moral and ethical conduct. Such religious and rhetorical education was alien to the people as it was designed to prepare priests and serve the upper classes. The contributions of the *conquistadores* through the 18th Century and until the era of independence included Iberian educational institutions, the addition of the Spanish and Portuguese languages, the Latin culture and value system, and Catholicism. Thus, the initial intrusion into the New World established the basic patters of education as well as political, economic, and social institutions and practices.

Latin American independence followed the French invasion into Spain and Portugal, finding all countries except Brazil with political, organizational, and economic problems which overshadowed the development of educational systems. This period, often referred to as the era of the dictators (1821-1910) was marked by the fear of enlightening the masses through education, the sending of children of elite families to France or Spain to be educated, and the continuation of an industrial and technological lag as many of the countries assumed an economic role as exporters of raw materials to the United States and Britain. Although Mexico, Argentina, and Chile began educational programs during the 19th Century, it was not until the early years of the 20th Century that substantial development occurred.

Domingo Faustino Sarmiento, of Argentina and Chile, was among the individuals who made important contributions to the educational systems of these countries during the 19th Century. Sarmiento, for example, was the principle catalyst to universal, compulsory, and free primary education in Argentina in the late 1800's, a pattern which he brought with him after several years of world travel and the friendship of Horace Mann.

The major influence on Latin American education in the 19th Century came from France. As a result, most educational systems became more highly centralized with strong emphasis placed on an academic curriculum of an encyclopaedic nature geared toward the study of Europe rather than the New World. Building on the French influence and turning toward the United States, most countries had taken control of their educational systems from the Church and had legislated into existence a system of primary education by the turn of the Century.

Foreign models of education gave way to a more national consciousness and introspection concerning the nature of each country's problems as a result of the Mexican Revolution of 1910. At the end of World War I, Europe was impoverished and remote and the United States gradually took over many of the prior European contacts with Latin America. The result was the substitution of English for French in the schools and the inclusion of North American texts and some pedagogical and school practices. Between the 1920's and the late 1960's, the dependence on the United States for technical assistance in the educational arena increased throughout Latin America. From tests and measurements and guidance counseling, to the administration and organization of schools and the curriculum itself, North American models and practices were diffused throughout the region. Although the current pattern of dependence on the United States has changed somewhat as a result of growing nationalist movements in Latin America, there appears to be a considerable educational influence and borrowing from among North American patterns.

This brief historical outline points to the well established importation of educational innovation and change in Latin America. Iberian, French, and United States influence through political and economic forces has accompanied the growth and development of educational systems which, in their composite forms, have often emerged as confused and contradictory. Thus, in Latin America today one finds a mixture of educational practice and a tradition of dependence upon outside sources of technical and financial assistance. The problems and issues of North American education abroad must be placed into this context since it is the history of Latin American international relationships which has supported the reliance upon foreign innovations and the consequent lack of institutions in existence in Latin America which correspond to the region's particular socio-cultural needs and directions.

Technical and Financial Assistance

What has been referred to here as Latin American dependence should not be interpreted as a lack of understanding or a lack of analytical capabilities among Latin American educators. University professors, ministerial officials, and other educational leaders and decision-makers in Latin America are knowledgeable about the educational and social problems which face them and are likewise interested in and capable of providing potential solutions. What they often lack are the financial resources to carry out their ideas and plans. Yet, bilateral technical assistance, along with loan and grant agreements, are products of the biases of each of the participating members and inevitably carry with them constraining elements which tend to favor the agency most closely associated with the source of funds.

The United States is represented in Latin America through a large number of private and governmental agencies whose major concern is Latin American socio-economic development. These include private foundations representing the business and philanthropic communities (Ford, Rockefeller) and governmental technical assistance offices associated with the United States State Department among others. As is common elsewhere, the offices in Latin America associated with the United States government represent the means for acquiring technical assistance and capital investment resources. It is from these government offices that North American university and private education corporations derive their contract funds to carry out education and development activities in Latin America. It is also through such agencies that loan funds are often secured from such agencies as the World Bank and the Inter-American Development Bank.

Since technical assistance and capital investment agreements involve financial resources, Latin American educational decision-makers must remain in close contact with either United States Government and technical assistance missions, or with such agencies as UNESCO and the Organization of American States. In the case of U.S. assistance, the particular educational problems in a host country are identified and the appropriate United States development officer and the Latin American official begin to prepare the necessary documentation for the analysis of the problem area, the presentation of alternative solutions, and an eventual proposal for funding. If the proposal is identified as a sound investment, funds may arrive two or three years later. Often during this process, specialists from North America are involved as consultants. These individuals have traditionally been selected for their expertise in working with educational problems in the United States, with the assumption that such organizational, technical, and curricular expertise has developed from a common base thus making the elements applicable for cross-cultural, development problems.

The Uninitiated and Unknowledgeable "Expert" in Technical Assistance

Such assumptions often mean problems for the uninitiated North American educator. Although visiting schools, watching teachers and students in classrooms, and talking with ministerial officials in many Latin American countries could give one the impression that educational problems are universal, such is actually the case at only certain levels of abstraction. It is true that elements such as delivery, message, and receiving systems are universal when one is faced with designing or altering an educational system. Yet, the social, political, cultural, and economic patterns which constrain and support such systems, together with the way each system is potentially able to answer host country educational concerns, is different and most often situationally specific.

The problem here concerns the North American who fails to speak the host country language, is unaware of cultural and demographic realities, and has not studied the local political processes. Without such basic understandings, the foreign consultant can only offer the technical expertise; he cannot act as a clinician to translate such expertise into practical problem solving in the Latin American context. One way to portray such technical assistance activity would be to imagine an invitation being extended to a group of Latin Americans to visit the United States to provide advice on some aspect of primary school education. Assume that they speak no English, have never studied the administrative organization of such schools, know nothing of how schools are financed, and are unaware of how teachers are trained, retrained, hired, or fired, etc. It is easy to see that such individuals would be of little use to the North Americans; the most they could offer, assuming some translation was possible, would be an indication of how they solved a similar problem given their own local conditions and constraints.

The notion of the "uninitiated" technical assistance "expert" causes the downfall of many bilateral and multilateral agreements. As is the case with the hypothetical Latin American experts, many technical specialists from the United States have little more to offer than some indication of how they have solved what appears at one level of abstraction as a similar problem. Such solutions are either forced into the existing educational system, or the host country educational system is altered in order to accept the innovation.

Exporting North American Educational Practice

One of the recent examples of such complete alteration involves the so-called comprehensive high school of the United States. This multi-track institution has been exported to Latin America to replace secondary schools which have traditionally been separated by function, e.g., academic, technical-vocational, agricultural, etc. As a result of United States technical assistance and World Bank Loans several countries have now adopted the comprehensive high school organizational and curricular pattern. Whether such institutions prove to be cost-effective, efficient, and able to respond to local social conditions will take time and will demand considerable analysis and research — something which has been sadly neglected by bilateral and multilateral agencies in the past.

The comprehensive high school is only one example of a long list of innovations which are tied to a United States pattern which may or may not have proved beneficial in their original North American habitat. An observer sometimes receives the impression that North American educators are selling their own patterns to others as a panacea for the myriad problems inherent in social change. For example, there is the "hardware" man who sells television, satellites and teaching machines; the "software" salesman who builds upon North American teacher-student classroom behavior to sell discovery learning and instructional objectives; and the administrative expert who sells decentralization and operations research systems. Even if one could turn to evidence that such innovations have proved to be beneficial in the United States, it is certainly reasonable to question their effectiveness in the Latin American context.

Latin American Reliance and the Move Toward Independence

Since the North American consultant is hired as a short-term specialist, and because he is a member of a team of such individuals, his advice is often written in a report which he leaves with the longer term North American and Latin American staff in the host country. Such reports are often filled with assumptions based on particular North American value premises and in and of themselves are not particularly useful documents for applied development programs. In effect, such reports need to be screened for their potential contribution and translated into concepts which have meaning for the host country staff. Because such visiting experts are housed in a hotel with their North American colleagues and because only a very few speak sufficient Spanish to be at ease professionally, what often occurs is a good opportunity for discussion among North Americans but little opportunity for interaction with the host country staff who will be charged with operating the new program.

Why do Latin Americans continue the reliance upon North American experts if the picture I have sketched approaches the reality of technical assistance activities? Assuming that Latins are conscientiously attempting to seek solutions to their educational problems, I believe there are at least two reasons for this dependence. First, and foremost, there is a tradition of accepting foreign advice in Latin America. Although I see this orientation changing through increased attention being placed on nationalistic concerns by inward looking leadership, I believe that Latin Americans associate North

American educational practices with the latest in advanced industrial technology and are interested in acquiring the status symbols which represent current educational practice. Secondly, and much more pragmatic, is the scarcity of funds which plague the majority of Latin American nations. They have no choice; they must seek external financial assistance. They are willing to trade their autonomy in terms of decision- making for such funds while quite clearly aware of the fact that this means accepting, at least in part, the advice of foreign specialists.

I believe that technical assistance activity should not be associated with particular solutions to educational problems as it has in the past. Such programs would serve the interests of the relatively underdeveloped societies more if they were to place attention on the analysis of educational problems and a discussion of all of the alternative solutions to a particular problem which have been used throughout the world. This analytical alternative to traditional technical assistance would leave Latin Americans with a set of tools and techniques for studying their own problems, and a set of alternative solutions enabling them to develop a syncretic construct which might meet the particular conditions and constraints of the local setting. The objective is to promote a transition from dependence to independence enabling the United States to refrain from exporting its prepackaged solutions and permit Latin Americans to analyze and propose solutions to their own educational problems relying upon such international agencies as the World Bank for financial resources. Such technical assistance practices will demand a different type of "expert" from the United States. He would need to be aware of a wide variety of alternative solutions to educational problems in the development context and necessarily be well grounded in the cultural realities of the host country where he would work.

It is probable that this alternative technical assistance activity is inevitable given the increasing nationalistic posture of the various Latin American societies. There appears to be considerable concern among at least some leaders that continued dependence will lead to a greater homogenization of cultures within the hemisphere. In education, this is occurring through the mass media, including film, television, and most recently satellite communications, resulting in increased consumerism of North American products.

Since formal schooling can only reflect the cultural norms which exist in the wider society, the future of educational dependence will inevitably rest with the attitudes and values of Latin Americans. There is some hope that North Americans and Latin Americans are beginning to heed the dangers inherent in promoting economic development at the cost of cultural integrity. Although not aligned with the education sector *per se,* a new United States government foundation was recently started that provides some hope for the future. The Inter-American Foundation is a non-profit, government corporation designed to assist Latin American development goals through grants and loans for social action projects at the grass roots level. The Foundation is novel in that it does not normally provide technical assistance through foreign universities, in fact any involvement by other institutions is based upon a collaborative, counterpart relationship. The Foundation responds quickly to host country initiative and has no permanent staff in Latin America. Funding is carried out with little fanfare and reduces dramatically the lag time associated with other development agencies in awarding grants and loans. In addition, the Inter-American Foundation is committed to evaluating its social action projects in order to learn more about social change in Latin America. The results of such evaluations are then disseminated to others within the hemisphere who have need for such information.

The Inter-American Foundation is truly novel in terms of its approaches to development issues and warrants considerable attention during the coming years in order to test its basic "response" rather than "directed" orientation to Latin American initiatives. Such an approach is a significant step in the direction of enabling Latin Americans to control their own destiny and to remove at least some of the constraints mentioned earlier regarding United States involvement in the international assistance arena.

Chapter 14

THE EUROPEAN EDUCATIONAL REFORM PROCESS

Val D. Rust

European education during the past decade has been characterized by extensive reform. The organizational structures and instructional modes which are coming into being are the result of a growing tendency for careful and coordinated planning. A number of countries have established curriculum research and evaluation schemes where the major share of this planning is expected to take place. Government agencies, private and autonomous foundations, scholarly research and training institutions, as well as individual schools in these countries, have become a coordinated network with the intention that appropriate reforms will be planned, adopted, and carried out. However, distinctive working relationships have evolved between these groups in different national settings.

Educational change agents are confronted with the task of establishing a mechanism to insure that plans are adopted and carried out at every institutional level. For example, nationally sponsored curricular programs must filter through regional, local, and individual school offices, and eventually be put into practice by the classroom teacher if the national program is to reach the individual pupil. Such programs are often blocked or distorted by officials or other personnel who try to subvert them. To offset such attempts, a vast supervisory and inspection network is often established to insure cooperation and compliance by officials and teachers.

The major obstacle to pedagogical and curricular reform has inevitably been the teacher. The practical instructional understanding of teachers provide needed direction during the formative stages of planning and curriculum development, and the teacher must either cooperate or be compelled to learn and execute the tasks expected of her or the rest of the planning process is of little value. For this reason it is essential that change agents understand the alternative modes of joint participation in educational reform which teachers might assume as well as their possible consequences. This paper will focus on the role of the teacher in France, Spain, West Germany, Sweden, Denmark, and England with respect to the working relationships that exist between the teacher and the other agencies and institutions involved in the reform process. Three broad patterns have emerged in Western Europe which might be characterized in the following ways: (1) Reforms are initiated at higher levels of government where the task of teachers is to act as agents of the government in carrying out the reforms. (2) Teachers form one group among many who participate in a conjoint effort at every stage in the reform process. (3) Reforms are primarily school-based and teacher-controlled. Essentially, these three patterns are ideal characterizations and a number of variations can be found within each pattern.

Teacher as Agent

The most pervasive, though by no means the most successful pattern of working relationships, is evident in countries with a highly centralized administrative tradition such as France and Spain. In these countries the teacher is viewed as an agent through which reforms might be realized. In Spain, reform is a matter of national governmental policy and is centered in the Ministry of Education. A research arm of the ministry, the National Research Center for the Development of Education, was established in 1969 to coordinate research of educational institutions and to promote the reforms. The center collaborates with high level international agencies such as UNESCO and the Ford Foundation for technical assistance and financial support of curricular and methodological reforms. The products of the National Research Center and the scholarly institutions will be transmitted to regions and adopted at schools that have been specified as demonstration institutions. As the programs are shown to be successful in the demonstration schools an expanding number of schools are chosen to participate. The role of the Spanish teacher in these efforts is two-fold. First, groups of teachers are brought to the National Research Center and participate in the actual development of instructional units which are exportable to the demonstration schools. Second, the National Research Center has also embarked on a large scale teacher reorientation program to insure that teachers are able to handle the technology involved in the programs.

The role of the teacher in France is much like that of Spain, though the French have decentralized their activities in that twenty regional research and development centers have been established which correspond in large measure to the Educational Research Department of the central ministry. These centers were set up to insure that local and regional offices which are responsible for carrying out reforms shall participate in the initial planning stages. All reforms, whether they be curricular, structural, or methodological, are tightly organized from school-based teams consisting of teachers and specialists representing different administrative levels. Following the groping trial-and-error stage characteristic of any new development, the innovation proceeds through increasing levels of formalization. These projects are closely monitored by the research and development centers and even though interest from a number of schools is often present, participation is allowed only if the school is selected and properly inducted into a project. Personnel from colleges and universities cooperate in the projects. They are usually charged with coordination responsibilities within and between teams and for retraining teachers in participating schools. Inherent in this scheme is coherent planning and implementation of reforms throughout the entire French educational system.

Both in France and in Spain, certain teachers are involved in the actual development of programs. The Spanish temporarily elevate certain teachers to a higher stratum within the bureaucracy in order for them to develop instructional materials, whereas the French teachers in the participating schools form an integral element of planning, development, and adoption of programs. As programs in France move to higher levels of formalization, teachers in newly participating schools are no longer involved in formation of policy and direction of reforms. However, they are expected to act as agents in carrying out the programs. For most of the teachers in both Spain and France, reforms will consist largely in developing the professional skills necessary to carry out the programs that others have set in motion as well as acting to help incorporate formalized programs into their own schools.

Since West Germany is administratively much more complex than Spain and France, it is somewhat difficult to outline the procedures through which reforms are adopted, though the end result is that teachers are more often than not expected to act as agents to carry out reforms that come from the various state ministries of education. Education is controlled by the different states in West Germany although two national education bodies now exist. The various states have maintained a Standing Conference of Ministers of Education for approximately two decades and this body has acted as a coordinating and policy making agency. In the post World War II era the Standing Conference of Ministers acted as a stabilizing body, but since the mid-sixties it has embarked on a major effort to initiate educational experimentation. In 1970 the federal government of West Germany established the Federal Council on Education which makes recommendations on the national level but which has no legal powers. The Standing Conference of Ministers of Education has no connection with this new council, thus affairs at the national level are confused.

The Standing Conference of Ministers of Education has maintained a strong hold on all innovation, and insists that experiments which depart from the basic structure of the state educational systems require "prior recommendation" of the Standing Conference of Ministers of Education. In other words, innovation takes place when the school officials recommend that it take place. One innovative recommendation which originated from the Federal Council on Education was that experimental programs for five-year-olds be instituted, and three states including Hesse, adopted this proposal. In Hesse a limited number of schools initially were selected with less than half a dozen new schools allowed to adopt the program each year, although that number will increase geometrically toward the later stages of the fifteen-year project. Although certain schools have asked to participate, they are often selected because of other social forces such as an interested town council or an active parent group. The individual teacher in the participating school has little choice but to accept her new role though she is provided with a full array of administrative and in-service support in order to make the adjustment.

It is clear that the main task of most of the teachers in France, Spain, and West Germany shall be to obtain the skills necessary to carry out reform programs. Consequently, institutionalized reform organs are being set up in these lands which concern themselves specifically with the reorientation of teachers and the development of study courses for retraining programs. In the Netherlands, which also treats the teacher as a government agent to carry out reforms, special institutions representing general, Catholic, and Protestant schools have been set up to carry out pedagogic and curriculum innovation. These centers are designed to cooperate with educational organizations and schools in promoting reform programs, but their main efforts have been directed toward teacher reorientation. Originally, the centers organized conferences and correspondence courses, but these proved to be unsatisfactory and the centers have recently concentrated on organizing demonstration schools and lessons.

Elsewhere, teacher reorientation programs in certain countries are largely extensions of traditional in-service activities. Such is the case in West Germany. For example, the Rhineland-Palatinate, a new state institute for in-service education has just been completed. This institute provides two- to five-day courses throughout the year whereby teachers might on a voluntary basis with no personal expense, learn the latest curricular developments in their field of study as well as general didactic studies.

Teacher as Partner

The second pattern of institutional coordination of reforms is observable in Scandinavian countries, and it has resulted in greater compatibility in working relationships between teachers and the other components of the reform network. A concerted attempt is made on the part of Swedish officials to include teacher groups in the development of local and national policy formation, although teachers do not view their role as representing a special interest power block but consider themselves as one element in a coordinated and fused national course of action. In other words, teachers are not simply technical implementers of policy but are contributors in a vital and often decisive manner to policy decisions themselves.

Sweden, though administratively centralized, has initiated lively discussion of educational problems and has disseminated detailed information from all interested groups and in the process has been able to maintain broad consensus about reforms. Teachers are generally sympathetic with national goals, although they have expressed growing frustration that they are insufficiently prepared to cope with the reforms they helped set in motion.

In the middle of the last decade the Swedish National Board of Education initiated a program whereby educational institutions conduct courses to help teachers deal more adequately with new curricular and structural reforms in schools. Each of the twenty-four counties in Sweden has established a corps of itinerate consultants who divide their time between classroom teaching and advisory work with teachers in the schools of the county. All teachers are freed from regular instructional duties several days each year in order to participate in obligatory training programs which are run by these itinerate consultants. If a training session involves larger teacher groups they will be given provision to travel to a designated location at state expense. A full array of voluntary in-service courses for teachers is also provided during vacations or after school.

In Denmark, one mechanism to help teachers cope more adequately with reforms can be found in the form of school centers. Jointly financed since 1967 by the government and local authorities, each of these centers employs approximately half a dozen full- and part-time educators who coordinate a full range of activities, namely: use of new teaching aids and equipment, discussion of current pedagogical problems, displays, lectures, and the more traditional courses. The center brings all its resources to bear in assisting the staff of any school which is revising its curricular program. Each of the twenty-five counties in Denmark sponsors school centers and they serve as a meeting place in which central administrators confer with county officials concerning educational policy deliberations.

Teacher as Leader

Centers are not only found in Denmark, but they have recently become an integral part of the educational scene in England. The English teachers' centers form the backbone of still a third mode of reform in Europe. For it is in these institutions that teachers themselves are assuming the major responsibility for bringing about fundamental change. Though support from British national bodies, foundations, research institutions, and local agencies has been just as intense as in the other countries we have looked at, these bodies have assumed the role as support agents for the individual teachers. Even though Royal commissions have been influential in swaying public policy and training colleges have long encouraged new practices and attitudes, the primary source for change must be attributed to those individuals who are working with the children in the schools. Such an observation should not imply that teachers were either prepared or capable of undertaking such radical reforms alone. The national task was not viewed as one of curriculum and methodological reforms alone, but involved the creation of a climate in which teachers themselves would critically reassess their ideas about educational practice and be willing to reorient personal values and attitudes. The institutional answer to this requirement came in the form of teachers' centers which have come into full-scale existence because of several forces at play in reforms.

In 1964 the Schools Council was established by the Department of Education and Science. Its purpose was to facilitate communication and cooperation pertaining to curriculum and examinations on the national level. The basic premise on which it has functioned has been that individual schools have the fullest possible measure of responsibility for their own work. Curricula and teaching methods evolve from the school staff itself to meet the needs of their own pupils.

Besides the Schools Council, other national development projects played a role in the establishment of teachers' centers. The Nuffield Foundation, for example, had been frustrated in its attempts to help teachers incorporate new curricular practices in French, mathematics, and the sciences because teacher interest and enthusiasm in new ideas, following reorientation courses, was short-lived. The Nuffield Foundation began to insist that if a local education authority wished to participate in their reorientation courses it must be willing to provide facilities where teachers might collaborate with each other on a regular basis after the course was completed. This incentive contributed further to the establishment of teachers' centers.

· National developments were not the sole contributors to the formation of teachers' centers; local initiative was equally responsible. For example, teachers themselves initiated curricular reforms and soon received institutional support for their designs. Local education authorities initiated curriculum development groups and adopted the Schools Council policy that development would remain school-based and teacher-controlled. Several local education authorities set aside facilities for these groups to work and eventually created new positions for wardens and other personnel to run the centers.

In 1968, less than four years after the formation of the Schools Council, over 300 teachers' centers were established in England and Wales. In a survey completed in May 1971, the number of centers listed by local education authorities had reached 473.

Teachers' Centers have become a focal point for concentrating the resources and energies of all the agencies involved in school reform. Multi-purpose centers are intended to serve a variety of needs within a local education authority. Many centers are subject specific and concentrate on such topics as reading, English, science, and mathematics, while others address themselves to critical social problems such as urban schooling or immigrant needs. During a given term dozens of meetings, programs, and workshops are conducted at the various centers. Since participation is voluntary, these activities are designed to address themselves to the specific interests of teachers.

Conclusion

As we have seen, three broad patterns of curriculum planning and design have emerged in Western Europe. The role of the teacher in the reform process differs significantly from country to country. Because the reforms differ markedly in terms of national commitment, duration of the reform period, and availability of resources, one would be ill-advised to make a final judgment at this point in time about the relative merits of these approaches. It is advisable for Americans to become acutely aware of the alternatives available as they consider courses of action in their own country.

In the United States curriculum reform during the past several years ostensibly has been the primary responsibility of Research and Development Centers and Regional Laboratories, which have been financed by the Federal Government. Each center has been charged with a specific responsibility such as the Center for the Study of Evaluation, or the Center for Research and Development in Teaching. As a center discovers new truths, these are disseminated to the field where enlightened professionals will pick them up. In case this does not occur, certain state legislatures are mandating that local school districts adopt programs and procedures. Teachers have been able to adjust fairly quickly to this course of action because it is not unlike traditional curriculum development practices in America.

Prior to the period in which the Federal Government supported educational research and development, state education departments and local school districts had generally adopted a trickle-down policy with regard to innovation. That is, supervisors and experts in the bureaucracy would develop syllabi and curricular programs that were imposed on the teacher. At best, the teacher was consulted as to the type of program to be adopted. In-service training was usually conducted in cooperation with a near-by teachers college or university, and materials for the programs were developed by commercial companies competing for their share of the market. All of these forces defined and limited the role of the teacher as an important agent for change.

On the surface such a practice was justified on the basis that curriculum planning and design were too complex and time-consuming for the ordinary teacher to engage in. This process is most difficult and it requires an enormous effort on the part of individuals. Time and effort are compounded when teacher-based reform is viewed on a national level. Systems analysis would surely indicate that curriculum reform is more efficient when conducted in central research and development institutes which are staffed by technical experts. From a strategic point of view, the least efficient process imaginable would be reform action which is initiated, planned and instituted at the local level, which in this case is the individual teacher or teaching team. The efficiency of the curriculum development process is not the ultimate criterion of success; it must be the performance-change of the teachers and, ultimately, of their students.

The American record of genuine educational change is not impressive. In the past several decades curriculum programs, on the surface, have changed radically. In spite of these apparent reforms, conditions in the classrooms have remained quite stable. It is becoming increasingly clear that successful reforms require joint coordination and participation from a wide array of forces in society. Since teachers constitute such an integral part of successful reform, some mechanism must be established whereby teachers will be willing to cooperate in the programs, and resources must be provided to help teachers orient themselves to new skills and attitudes. European reforms provide the American teacher with some alternative approaches to this problem.

PART III

RECRUITMENT, TRAINING, AND EVALUATION IN UNITED STATES OVERSEAS EDUCATION

We do not have an accurate and current count of the numbers of educators who serve overseas at a given time. However, by including those in the dependent and international schools, the overseas branches of colleges and universities, U.S. employees of UNESCO and throwing in a few extra, we arrive at a figure approaching 25,000. In any case, there are a lot of American educators outside their homeland. As we all know, people comprise most organizations, especially in education, which as a field employs one of the largest contingents of professional-level people in most countries of the world.

Thus far in this book, we have presented some of the conditions, motivations, and problems which are a realistic part of the life of an overseas educator. We have attempted to project the concept that we need our very best teachers, administrators, consultants, and support staffs abroad. They are the chief communicators of one of the world's major cultures. They are ambassadors of the United States every time they speak with a foreign national. They have the responsibility to help shape the lives of American young people, and often the future leaders of other countries. The following chapters are targeted at considering the factors and the needs of proper selection, orientation and development of these educators, and measuring their impact overseas.

My own contribution is basically a review of the many processes of educator recruitment for overseas assignment by various agencies and organizations and of the difficulties which confront the educator who is about to or has recently returned from his overseas experience. Also included is a flow chart describing the specific steps taken in an educator's search for an overseas job and the overseas employer's talent search. There are several strong suggestions which are aimed at improving the recruitment and reentry processes of American educators who work abroad.

In the preparation of teachers to deal with what he terms "changes in life space" Asa G. Hilliard suggests a type of reformation. He advocates the necessity to provide an international and intercultural dimension in *all* programs of teacher training. He points to the personal values gained by the educator able to learn in an intercultural context. Using a page or two of description about his own experiences, he builds a rationale for program development along the lines of his recommendations.

John Bahner, who has assisted scores of overseas schools with administrative and in-service matters, builds one base of his chapter on the major issues of overseas school finance which greatly affects staffing patterns and school organization. All of these considerations are important for educators to recognize when planning employment abroad.

Additionally, the other base from which he writes is that of in-service education and the problems surrounding the continued enrichment of the skills and knowledge of educators. He also provides a specific example of a successful training model developed and proven to be quite effective by I/D/E/A/.

Not only is evaluation the watchword in American education in the United States, it has also crept overpoweringly into the vocabularies of those responsible for measuring the worth of what is taught; who the learners are; and how and how much they learn abroad. David Churchman, an experienced evaluator of overseas programs, uses four case studies to identify the various problems and factors which necessitate evaluation activity. These specific examples form the approach through which he presents various types of evaluation techniques and a model which has been extremely useful to those responsible for overseas educational programs.

Innovation and research have grown in importance in the rapidly changing field of education worldwide. In overseas schools in which Americans work, the participation of teachers in educational planning and program administra-ation warrants their development of knowledge and awareness of educational development and reform. That overseas educational activities do and will continue to exist warrants an essential concentration by educators and educational employers alike upon the screening, training, qualifications, conditions of service and opportunities that are of the highest merit possible.

Chapter 15

OVERSEAS EDUCATOR SEARCH AND RESCUE

William G. Thomas

From whence cometh the teachers, the administrators, librarians, counselors, residence advisors, and others who serve in American sponsored or affiliated educational programs abroad? Is there an overseas educator collection agency? An educational talent savings and loan organization for overseas acculturation? An international placement agency? Or, contrarily, are there a collection of small educational employment agencies and educational recruiters which identify overseas prospects for overseas programs much like the flesh peddlers of yore? In reality, a little of the first and a lot of the second forms of finding overseas educators exist. In fact, the recruitment of overseas educators is one of the most undernourished, diseased and neglected spheres of educational personnel identification and development; yet one of the most important. It is only overshadowed by the dismal situation faced by overseas educators who attempt to return to meaningful positions in the United States.

Some of the agents of overseas talent discovery are merely well-dressed procurers. Running educational employment "body shops," they have ·absolutely no knowledge of the actual needs and desired skills of employers. In a few instances, a computer performs the candidate-overseas job matching function. Some American community schools overseas consider placement papers sent to them solely from one or a very few fee-charging screening agencies or brokers. A set of autobiographical materials, letters of recommendation, and a brief half-to-one-hour interview (or none at all) judge a few fortunate souls to be qualified for educational positions in foreign places they have never seen with people they have never met. At worst, the situation is intolerable for all parties concerned (especially the children to be served). At best, there are difficulties of making important "people" decisions on the basis of limited information and very little personal interaction. There are many aspects of an educational position in a foreign culture which differ from a stateside situation; many immediate challenges (such as a political uprising, the closure of an embassy, the relocation of an overseas American business firm, etc.) which require immediate solutions; and more adjustment necessities.

Overseas educational positions are either well-kept secrets uncovered by only a few people or they are advertised far and wide. Postal services are inundated as job description flyers are reproduced, abstracted, made a part of educational job listings, transmitted, translated, and re-translated through a series of recipients, until finally reaching an interested party.

In short, between an overseas educational position opening and a talented, well-qualified person to fill that post there is a vast distance filled with piles of correspondence, countless disbursements of information, and numerous brokers, all over and above the miles which separate them. This paper is both a consideration of that distance and some ways in which it can be decreased.

To begin with, there are several categories into which educational programs may be placed in which Americans may be involved: United States Government-Affiliated Agencies, Overseas American Community Schools, International Schools, Religious-Sponsored Educational Organizations, National Educational Systems, and International Programs of Study Abroad. Since their methods of discovering skilled educational personnel are different, each is separately considered.

The United States Government has a large number of overseas educational programs: the Institute of International Studies (U.S. Office of Education), the Dependents' School System, the binational centers of the U.S. Information Agency, the activities of the Office of Overseas Schools (U.S. Department of State), and the Peace Corps, a Division of ACTION.

Within the Institute of International Studies, the Division of Foreign Studies is involved in the training of specialists in foreign studies and in research to support the activities of overseas American education. Individuals are recruited by virtue of expertise or prominence in a particular area, as well as through direct application. They are selected as to overseas need. Ordinarily, personal interviews are conducted.

The Division of International Exchange and Training, authorized by the Fulbright-Hayes Act, provides opportunites for qualified American teachers to teach for an academic year or to attend summer sessions abroad. Interested individuals apply in the early fall for positions to be filled during the following year. They are interviewed by fifty-nine volunteer committees of educators in forty-one states, Puerto Rico, and the District of Columbia. These committees send their recommendations to a Washington office, which makes final determinations on the basis of matched exchanges and available overseas posts.

The U.S. Department of Defense, Directorate for Dependents' Education, provides American-type elementary and secondary school curriculum for the minor dependents of military and civilian employees. This enormous school system is administered by the Army, Navy and Air Force, and coordinated through the Department of Defense. Applicants are ordinarily selected through computer-matching or, occasionally, when abroad, by personal interview.

Binational centers are private, autonomous organizations, which are governed by American residents and nationals of a host country and the United States. American educators are hired requisite to the nature of offerings in courses, seminars, lectures, movies, libraries, and other means of describing the American culture to those in other parts of the world. Employees are located through direct application and personal interview. They are given brief orientations in Washington, D.C., before assuming their overseas responsibilities.

The Peace Corps recruits teachers and administrators for its various programs by sending representatives throughout the U.S. to inform, screen and interview likely prospects. They also conduct briefings and training programs for successful volunteers and staff officers.

Elementary and secondary schools modeled around a typical American curriculum exist throughout the world. Such schools have been developed to serve the children of Americans who are employed overseas in either commercial or governmental capacities. They are located in such places as London, Guadalajara, Algiers, Barcelona, and Tokyo. They incorporate an American curriculum to make the transition easier for children to reenter stateside schools and to promulgate their cultural heritage. Recruitment for such schools is conducted in numerous ways. Some people are hired through direct candidate application and the screening of their placement materials. Others arrange for personal interviews while living in or visiting geographical areas in which schools are located. Referrals are also made to schools by such organizations as the International Schools Service, or resumés of qualified applicants may be forwarded by such bodies as the European Council on International Schools. Additionally, a number of American Community Schools publicize their personnel needs in the United States and send recruiters to interview the most likely candidates.

International schools attract children of many nationalities. Rather than following an American-type curriculum, they may incorporate a British system, a French lycée method, or blend a variety of educational patterns together to suit the needs of a multi-cultured and multi-ethnic student body. Such schools recruit staff from the host country as well as from those countries represented by their students. They use educational employee procurement processes much like the American community schools, while emphasizing diversity in the international heterogeneity of their staff.

Religious-sponsored educational organizations, such as the United Church Board for World Ministries, Catholic Orders, and the Wycliff Bible Translators use their affiliate churches and denominational bodies to promote their overseas needs for educators. There are other schools abroad which are of a Protestant or Catholic persuasion and follow similar use of affiliates. Such organizations largely prefer to have educators of their particular religious leanings instruct and work with their youth. They hire through referral from trusted colleagues, screening of direct application materials, or as the British term them, "milk runs" in the United States.

National educational systems such as the Ministries of Education in Zambia, German Landern, and Australian territories often look to the United

States for educational expertise in particular fields when their own educational manpower supply is deficient. Most of their hiring of Americans is accomplished through intermediaries, with well-documented backgrounds being reviewed and those with the "best papers" provided a job. In some cases, travel to and from the overseas location is also included. One usually sees one's employer and the working environment only upon arrival on the scene. Occasionally, broker organizations in the U.S. arrange to screen and interview prospective employees.

Educational programs of study and travel abroad abound. The Foreign Study League, Study Tours, and World Encounters, Inc. are examples of these organizations which conduct overseas educational tours and "short-stay" language, arts, and humanities programs in foreign lands. They employ American educators as teachers, tour guides, chaperons and sales representatives. Most of the hiring is accomplished on a personal contact and referral basis, with many of the organizations both advertising and recruiting likely prospects for national and regional educational conferences. Such gatherings range from those of the American Language Association to the California Junior College Association.

Even though numerous colleges and universities have expanded their educational horizons beyond the physical facilities of a central campus through establishing overseas branches for other than for their own faculty there are only a smattering of educational employment opportunities for well-qualified individuals. Certainly, it is most common for higher educational institutions to draw from their own human resources. Nevertheless, when they go to "the outside," they normally follow regular college recruitment practices, i.e., promote the jobs, review applications, and personally interview the best candidates.

Among overseas educational employers, there are also international organizations such as UNESCO, the Experiment for International Living and the International Labor Organization which seek out and employ or refer to foreign nations or organizations individuals with the potential to perform certain jobs. Often, this process is lengthy and complicated. With UNESCO, for example, each member country, after locating qualified candidates, recommends them to the Paris central agency, which in turn screens further and sends only the dossiers of the very best prospects to the country originating the request. Host country officials then make their choices and UNESCO liaison officials in the countries of the successful applicant inform a candidate of acceptance and initiate the international processes for his overseas involvement – if he is still available. Many international bodies merely serve as clearinghouses or brokers of information, forwarding resumés and applications to prospective educational employers.

The objective in all of the above cases is primarily to locate and employ the best person for every potential job. Why is it so difficult to achieve this objective?

Looking at the situation simultaneously from both sides, that of the prospective employer and the prospective educational employee, the educational recruitment process involves parallel steps (see Chart 1). The employer must: 1) recognize a staffing need; 2) prepare a description of the available position; 3) identify sources through which qualified candidates may be located; 4) provide position descriptions to appropriate individuals, agencies and organizations; 5) receive and review applications from interested educators; 6) obtain supportive materials on selected candidates; 7) conduct interviews (in some cases); 8) select an appropriate candidate; and 9) negotiate the acceptance of the candidate. The educator seeking an overseas position must: 1) recognize his/her own need for an overseas situation; 2) prepare a resume; 3) identify sources through which overseas jobs can be located; 4) arrange to receive position information; 5) apply for appropriate positions; 6) send supportive documentation; 7) participate in employer interviews (when possible) 8) become a selected candidate; and 9) negotiate a contract.

Each of these steps in the search for overseas educational talent and for employment situations is problem-laden for both parties. Let us consider them, one by one.

In Step 1, the real personnel need is not always recognized or it becomes a need for the wrong reasons (a personality conflict, the lack of subject breadth in a teacher, etc.). The type of person desired has not been discussed with parents, fellow teachers, students (in some cases) or school board or agency members. Does the need exist to resolve a problem which can be removed by the presence of a qualified person or will the problem remain even with a new staff member? Contrarily, what are the reasons the educator desires to work abroad? To make a contribution? To gain new knowledge and insights in another culture? To gather information and material to enliven a classroom upon his/her return? For renewal? These are better considerations than the "opportunity for travel," "getting away for a while," or "a change of climate."

In Step 2, the majority of educational position descriptions are totally inadequate. Instead of providing the full details of an educational position (duties, functions, activities, salary, benefits, transportation arrangements, housing, nature of the school, student body, staff and local community), such unimaginative educational job portrayals as "fifth grade teacher," "middle school principal," and "combined music instructor (instrumental, vocal and choral)–biology instructor" are examples of actual "full" descriptions which have been advertised far and wide. Few answer the essential questions of *why* the job? *What* are the qualifications and duties? *Where* will the work take place? *How* is the compensation system? *When* will the various phases of the recruitment and selection process occur? A position description should serve as a plan for a person, a plan to help him/her to determine whether or not a

CHART 1

PARALLEL TRACKS OF RECRUITOR AND RECRUITEE

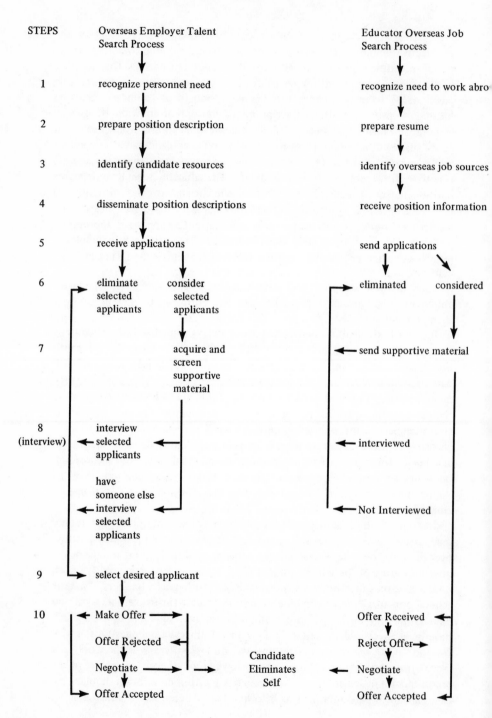

STEPS   Overseas Employer Talent
Search Process

Educator Overseas Job
Search Process

1   recognize personnel need   recognize need to work abro

2   prepare position description   prepare resume

3   identify candidate resources   identify overseas job sources

4   disseminate position descriptions   receive position information

5   receive applications   send applications

6   eliminate selected applicants   consider selected applicants   eliminated   considered

7   acquire and screen supportive material   send supportive material

8 (interview)   interview selected applicants   interviewed

have someone else interview selected applicants   Not Interviewed

9   select desired applicant

10   Make Offer   Offer Received

Offer Rejected   Reject Offer

Negotiate   Candidate Eliminates Self   Negotiate

Offer Accepted   Offer Accepted

match exists. Accurate, fully-detailed position descriptions eliminate the "shoppers" from the serious seekers.

The educator's resumé of description must be even more informative than a job description. It represents him/her in his/her physical absence. The resumé must thoroughly review one's academic and employment background, one's skills and interests, and provide insights as to one's capabilities and adaptability. Excellent resumés stand out uniquely.

Perhaps Step 3 contains the most pitfalls. You must get to the "right" places to locate the "right" people if you are an overseas employer. A few outstanding agencies cater to recruitment needs of educational organizations abroad. They are also rare. Others have neither the contacts, the coverage, nor the competency to find qualified applicants. Many are private educational employment agencies to which few quality educators would turn for assistance. By far the best programs through which teachers and administrators can be identified for overseas elementary, secondary, and higher institutions are college and university placement and career planning centers. They are the best equipped, and staffed, and cheapest means through which educational personnel can be found.

So it is with educators looking for overseas jobs. Should I list only with the International Schools Service? (A good service.) Shall I contact overseas schools and organizations directly? What are the best places where I can register to locate a position? Which friends should I inform of my interest and availability? Here again, colleges and universities are the best bets. For example, over 80 registrants of UCLA's Educational Careers Center accepted overseas positions through the direct involvement of the Center's staff. One should turn every stone when seeking an overseas position.

Step 4 depends largely on Step 3. Not only should the overseas employer send position announcements to stateside agencies, colleges and universities, but to former teachers, affiliates, school or organizational alumni and their parents, and to those professional organizations which have journals, newsletters, and/or placement services. Accordingly, the overseas job searcher must throughly cover the contents of publications and announcements which might identify available overseas posts and locate overseas educators who may have recently returned from abroad or who are on study or relaxation excursions for pertinent information.

Step 5, the initial consideration of applicants, involves what is frequently known as "paper screening." The applicant must realize that he/she is fully judged on the basis of a well developed letter of application and an even better developed resumé. The overseas educational employer, these days, observes the qualifications for a job rising with each batch of new applications. Instead of the best candidate having a master's degree (which was advertised), many have the doctorate. Advertising for a minimum of two years teaching experience, it is found that many applicants have ten or more years of solid teaching behind them. A premium is placed on the quality of one's degrees; academic major and minors; work experience, both within and outside of education; ability to do something, to contribute rather than merely filling a space; and uniqueness, the things which make one different.

Quite ordinarily, many applications will be unsolicited, sent by individuals who do not know, but hope a position might exist. Those who have taken the time to inquire about a possible opportunity should be acknowledged whenever possible. Good manners are also good public relations.

Many overseas employers neglect to take Step 7; so do many applicants. The collecting of supportive documentation as to a person's writing ability, corresponding with current and former employers and colleagues, and other examples of his/her work, are essential to long-distance employment considerations. Overseas employers should insure that they have more information than an autobiographical resumé which a person has prepared and recommendations which have been solicited by candidates. Applicants should prepare accurate documentation of their accomplishments and thorough information about who might be contacted to reinforce their candidacy.

In Step 8, some type of interview is implied. An overseas employer may make an annual trek to the United States to visit with prospective candidates or a stateside-residing representative may accomplish this essential task. Overseas educational employment is one of the few professional fields in which the prospective employer and employee may never meet until the employee arrives on the scene. Interviews should not be one-way communications. They should flow in two directions. One chooses a position, just as one is selected. If an educator is overseas for one reason or another, arranging for an on-site interview is a must. If he/she is not, some type of interview with some type of representative is also a must. There are just too many important questions about curriculum, teaching methods, the educational environment, the problems, and the positive elements to wait until one finds oneself captured in a miserable situation for a year or more.

Step 9 is like the final stage of the decision-making process – "selecting the appropriate decision." Through a series of screening activities, you have identified the person you want to fill the position in question. This is usually the most difficult part of the process. Criteria, perhaps even the employment situation itself, have changed; so have your ideas on who can do the best job.

Step 10 is making and receiving the offer itself. An offer should be clear and direct. It should indicate the major elements of consideration: salary, perquisites, responsibilities and pertinent dates. Many offers are vague, evasive, hardly believable. Give a person something to hang his/her hat on! An offer can be rejected, accepted or negotiated. There is nothing wrong with one making counter offers or proposals to a contract. It is best that what is expected by both parties is known to both parties; that way they are both as satisfied as possible. Include also, the procedures which are to be followed if either party does not fulfill his/her end of the contract.

All of the above represent the "search" part of the overseas educator situation. What about the "rescue" part?

Once ensconced in an overseas job, the educator (so we hope the story goes) has a pleasurable experience, relates well to the foreign culture, gains new educational and human insights, and looks forward to returning to the United States to share his/her wealth of knowledge with others. For those who have taken leaves of absence or are on sabbaticals from their home institutions — be they elementary, secondary, or higher schools — returning to an awaited job at home is not a problem. They have left their bases covered. However, to the person who has overstayed his/her leave or never had one (and there are many in this category, especially American community and dependent school administrators and long-term teachers), the opportunities at home appear to be bleak indeed. Lacking proper credentials in some cases, often out of touch with certain new administrative or teaching methodologies; i.e., P.P.B.S. (Program Planning and Budget System), C.A.I. (Computer Assisted Instruction), and other novel entries in the educational race, thousands of miles away from interview opportunities, a large group of disoriented Americans are scattered in both highly populated and remote islands of isolation from job opportunities in their native country. Do I stay overseas and become an expatriate? Do I return home and take the chance that someone will hire me? Can I afford to work on a doctorate? Each case is different. Yet, such are the plights of American educators overseas which must be resolved.

Now we have gone full circle. We have considered the "search"; we have briefly looked at the "rescue." How can this imperfect process be improved upon?

New techniques, methods, processes and systems must be conceived both to get our best educators overseas and to bring them back when they are ready. For example, why can't the Fulbright Teacher Exchange officials share their dossiers on the approximate 5,000 teachers who are annually interviewed throughout the United States (with the blessings of their local school districts) with the dependent, American community and International schools? Why can't the dependent schools identify talent via their computers and have competent educators in various sectors throughout the United States interview them or involve the interviewers who assist the Fulbright Teacher Exchange program? Why are there not regional centers, which could easily be developed by major universities' where outstanding educators interested in temporarily relocating overseas could be identified, job information disseminated, and interviews conducted. Why? Why not?

Well, for one thing, there is little or no contact between educational organizations with overseas endeavors. For the most part, they compete, rather than cooperate. As a matter of fact, there is not even a unifying organization between colleges and universities with overseas branches. Throughout the country, daily duplication occurs, checking travel rates, housing accommodations, arranging for insurance, and the like. Cooperation would cut costs, encourage the sharing of facilities and resources, and provide a forum for informational exchange.

What about recruitment? If an overseas educational employer wanted to thoroughly canvas prospective teachers in Los Angeles, for example, he/she would have to select from more than fifty colleges and universities, school systems, and organizations which could identify educators interested in going abroad. Here again, competition and lack of coordination breeds frustration and futility in identifying overseas prospects.

And what about teachers and administrators returning to the U.S.? The frantic letters, the desperate (and expensive) trips to interview for the few opportunities which arise, the frustration of no one wanting to learn about or valuing highly an educator's work abroad or its applicability to the new situation. What a waste!

With some recognition of the futility and impossibility of the situation, I offer the following, rather broad, suggestions in hopes that one or more kind souls in positions of prominence, people who really care about the welfare of American children overseas and those who teach them and administer to their needs, and those who share some of my concerns will do something about the "search and rescue" of overseas educators.

Suggestion One — That the United States Office of Education form an international committee or expand the responsibilities of an existing one to investigate the current status of the total American educational presence outside the continental United States and that this committee, representative of those organizations and agencies listed in this paper, develop a series of recommendations which would form cooperative relationships and subgroups, respectively, of elementary schools, secondary schools, higher educational institutions, foreign study and tour organizations, and other international education bodies. Such matters as curriculum, articulation, staffing, recruitment, educational innovation and inter-relationships would be paramount.

Suggestion Two — That twelve universities (the number is relative) in strategic locations throughout the United States form a consortium to identify, screen and interview prospective educators for overseas positions, to disseminate position information, and to coordinate the interview visits of overseas employers. Each of these universities would utilize already existing computer-matching systems to provide information about jobs to registrants and about registrants to prospective employers. Videotaped interviews would be developed of candidates for review of overseas employers. Overseas educational organizations would also develop films and videotapes and appropriate subjects. Placement files would be assembled and distributed from these centers.

The Centers would coordinate the reentry of overseas educators. Through the use of computer printouts to identify likely positions and the distribution of videotaped interviews, they would serve as advocate representatives of overseas teachers and administrators who wish to return to the United States.

Suggestion Three – That UNESCO or another international education body institute a forum to identify the immediate teacher, administrative, curriculum, and research needs of countries throughout the world, and that educators be identified and trained to resolve some of the problems of these countries. This would be of particular benefit to the current oversupply of teachers in the United States, many of whom could contribute mightily to peoples of foreign nations.

Suggestion Four – That every United States professional educational organization develop a committee on international educational personnel which would interact with other organizations to promote the dissemination of information about overseas employment opportunities and available overseas educators to its constituency.

These thoughts are not proferred with the assumption that all staffing problems of American-affiliated or sponsored overseas educational organizations will be solved through their incorporation. They are intended primarily to serve as a basis of discussion and further consideration.

If the suggestions result in a few closer relationships between organizations seeking personnel and those which can identify qualified educators, using computer-assisted information systems and videotape in selection processes, arranging campus interview visits on college and university campuses and wider dissemination of both job and candidate information, this particular "search and rescue" mission might be launched.

Chapter 16

IMPERATIVES FOR INTERCULTURAL TEACHER EDUCATION

Asa G. Hilliard

Sometimes I think that "movement" is the basic foundation of learning. When I say that, I am thinking of what has happened to me and what has seemed to happen to others when we have had to deal with changes in life space. No matter where a human being finds himself, he begins immediately to evolve an order that helps him to make sense of his new environment. Peter Berger has called this process, "The Social Construction of Reality." Each of us has a great deal to do with what we "see" and how we think the things which we see may work. While some of us are better than others in getting a dependable, replicable, or valid world together, we all come up with rough approximations of things as they really are. We develop incomplete systems, semi-descriptive names, makeshift concepts, and "explanations" that live to haunt us, especially if they are written down and are available to colleagues who in their cooler moments will find our thoughts to be at odds with their newer updated worlds. In the end, even though we all create partial worlds, there seems to be a tendency for us to regard them as the real one, with the "bugs" worked out. We get very comfortable in our world when we can predict things with a high level of accuracy. We even get protective of our seemingly dependable world and there is often an egotistic attempt to extrapolate our formulations to include worlds yet unknown. Ah yes, the settling in! The adrenalin ebbs. And then, abruptly, at times we find ourselves in another space, another house and the keys don't quite fit. We can deny or reject the new world or we can include it and rework our formulations. In the end it is likely that the new world will be somewhat bigger and somewhat different in shape. But, how will we be? Will we be ready for still another interruption?

This provincial view is common in the pages of history. Laws of motion, thermodynamics, gravity and others were eagerly sought and stated by physical scientists. Not to be outdone, our behavioral scientists were equally creative in developing laws of human behavior. It is interesting indeed that with more information about the world than ever before, we present theories rather than laws. *People who have had to accommodate many times do seem to be characterized by increasing modesty and something like a state of suspended tentativeness.*

I would guess that there are few among us here who have not had to deal with different life spaces. Undoubtedly, some have encountered only minimal differences while others have found themselves in radically different situations. In any case, I invite your introspection to recreate the beginning of

153

a particularly notable experience. Do you remember when you thought that you would never be able to eat that kind of food? Was there a time when the people who sounded different spoke so fast that you could only catch a few words in a sentence? Did you feel that you would never be able to learn that new dance that everyone else seemed to have down pat? Have you always felt the way you now feel about alcoholic beverages, pot? Would you teach your same class the same way if you had the chance to try again? Is your position the same as it always was on collective bargaining for teachers? No matter what the experience might have been at the beginning or now, the chances are very good that the encounter resulted in an expanded world for each of us.

Let me leave this line of thought for a few moments before returning to make some connections. I want to focus now on what I think out to be happening in the education of our nation's teachers. I don't think that it is too gross to say that it has been extremely difficult for our teacher education programs to escape the mire of *intellectualization about* teacher, student, and community actions. In a few programs, there is some departure from the basic seminar format in which students and teachers react to fuzzy recollections of one member or even more fuzzy projections of a member. Often in seminars, information is romanticized, exaggerated or otherwise distorted simply because that information comes through the verbalization of one person. These verbalizations are filtered through that person's perceptions and defenses. Some improvement in this situation has come with the use of videotaping, micro-teaching and systematic observations. However, there still tends to be too little hypothesis testing on a planned basis. Sociology, psychology, and philosophy are often separated from the field experience and, therefore, lack behavioral content. Anthropology is often left out altogether. Most teacher preparation programs give no more than a nod to this area which has developed some of the most fascinating and useful insights for teachers yet.

So far, I have only been talking about the necessity to develop a methodology for teacher education which provides the opportunity for concepts to be applied in real situations. There is still a finer cut to this whole approach. It has to do with the fact that teachers do not come to training as empty vessels. They come with their own very real psychologies, sociologies, anthropologies, and philosophies. However incomplete, naive, unsystematic these notions may be, *they are the bases for the operating hypotheses which the teacher will use.* In fact, the teacher may learn to verbalize the language of the classroom and continue to operate on the basis of his own deeply felt formulations. Still further, the teacher may not perceive the discrepancy between the actual theoretical base he uses and the one which he talks about. Therefore, teacher education priorities must include helping a teacher to discover his own *implicit operating framework,* helping a teacher to encounter alternative notions and to try some of them in real situations, and to develop ways of maintaining an awareness of the need for a continual integration of belief and behavior.

Let me try to nail this notion down with an example from my personal experience. California State University, San Francisco has operated an on-site, team taught, integrated content teacher education program for some time now. In addition, some faculty members follow a placement pattern which we call impacting. As many as thirty student teachers may be placed in the same school. I will not have time to describe the rationale for this. However, on one occasion it became necessary to move an entire group of student teachers from a school in which they had worked to a new school at the last moment. A number of difficulties were encountered in the move which were later overcome. However, it is interesting to note that the move offered an excellent opportunity for the application of sociological and psychological perspectives. What happens when a group of student teachers with their esprit, fixed aims (in this case the aims included trying out new methods of teaching reading), and pattern of working together? How will the established faculty in the new school and the community react, especially the community weary of "experimental programs" which use their children as guinea pigs? What about the school that lost the training program? Here were sociological processes in action. And yet, in this case, the opportunity was lost. The experience was so unsettling that no real reflection was done on the processes in progress by those faculty and students who were involved.

The Intercultural Base

I have been moving toward a rationale for the inclusion of an international/intercultural dimension in all programs for the preparation of teachers. This rationale is slightly different from the one that I hear most often which is based upon an end of preparing teachers to work overseas or with children in America who come from different cultures. Certainly these two goals for teacher preparation are necessary and highly desirable. However, I have come to believe that the best training for any teacher of any children or youth must include as much of an opportunity as is possible for the teacher to experience a different or expanded life space. The richness of professional operation in an intercultural situation offers unique possibilities for the development of sensitivity and flexibility in teachers.

I said earlier that movement seems to be a basic foundation of learning. When I think of teacher education, this seems especially true. Teachers today seem to come most often from the much maligned middle class. Our middle class pattern in America tends to be one of provincialism. *Often, the culturally deprived in our culture tend, unfortunately, to be our teachers!* Whether suburban or urban, associations tend to be narrow and intercultural contacts limited. At this point, my argument is not really social as much as professional. Intercultural settings provide the opportunity for pedagogical principles to stand in clear relief in a way that is impossible in a sterile monocultural environment.

When I go into a country which is new to me, I find that I go expecting to notice things. Little things which would go unnoticed at home are clearly defined. In fact, I am sometimes so prepared to find differences that it is possible that I will identify as different something that is an ordinary part of my home environment. I simply have not been prepared to pay attention to many things at home. I find that I am also more aware of myself in a strange context. Since I do not know appropriate ways of responding nor do I know the way in which my actions will be interpreted, I find that I am more considered in my actions and am more careful about clarity in communication. The motivation for being more aware is there. Even though new situations may be uncomfortable, I find that I feel that it is more tolerable to be in error in behavior. I believe that one becomes more free to analyze his own behavior since a person new to a culture is ignorant by definition. When there are real differences between behaviors, events, or things from my culture to the new, seeing them as contrasting extremes helps me to see the continuum more clearly. Perhaps the prime benefit of learning in an intercultural context is that I find that I am once again more aware of what it means to be a learner at the very same time that I am thinking of what I am able to do about teaching. At that point I am better able to view principles of human behavior from an internal as well as an external perspective.

Methodology

The kinds of things which I have just mentioned are best handled in a peer group situation. It is not automatic that an intercultural context alone will cause a person to be more aware, reflective, and open. It is important that one have peers who are experiencing the same condition. From a group one can get support, can check perceptions, can get non-threatening feedback on one's behavior, provided the proper facilitation is available.

I wish to be clear that there are many intercultural situations which are available to be used for teacher preparation purposes. International and inter-ethnic possibilities are obvious and certainly are the most desirable of all. In the absence of these, there are still age, economic, geographic, and other situations which can serve similar purposes. The important point is that the learner be placed in a condition which is as different as it can be from his own life space so that he must get into the process of organizing his world. At that point, guided inquiry into pedagogical analysis becomes more animated, more real, more grounded, and more effective.

Context

It is not enough for teachers to be in an intercultural situation if they only think in the usual ways about teaching and learning, even though the context itself may be rich, and unusual opportunities may present themselves. There are some special opportunities which the cross cultural context is ideally suited to offer. The program must be structured to take full advantage of these opportunities. I will spend a few moments sketching in the broad outline of these areas because they are treated inadequately in most programs that I know. Keep in mind the idea that each of these should be examined in a real context. Intellectual information is no substitute for the development of these concepts through one's life space.

Cognition

One day while I was working in Liberia, I had an occasion to be in a Loma village about two hundred miles into the interior and well off the main motor road. While sitting on the steps of a hut, seven or eight young boys about elementary ages came into the clearing. They spoke no English and I spoke no Loma. They seemed curious about me and walked in my direction. I had a small pen-sized microscope with me and pulled it from my shirt pocket. I sprinkled some sand on a plank and began to look at it through the microscope. Soon the boys were around me at a respectable distance obviously more curious now. After a few moments a small boy caught my eye and I knew he wanted to see. I passed the microscope to him silently and he took it eagerly and quickly began to peer through. He expressed surprise immediately and began to talk excitedly to the other boys. They pushed and shoved for a chance to look. Soon they were taking turns. After the fourth boy looked, the second boy reached down and pulled up a part of a weed. At once all boys seemed to want to try looking at the weed under the microscope. Then they began to bring all kinds of things to look at. Finally a large boy grabbed the microscope from another boy and put it to his eye and pointed in the direction of a tree in the distance. Here were boys with no formal schooling, who spoke no English, who had not used many technical tools if any, but who obviously were exhibiting rather naturally logical and complex mental operations. They recognized that the microscope made things appear different. Then logically, if sand is made bigger then other things should be made bigger (immediate inference). When the large boy looked at the tree, he appeared disappointed. He recognized apparently that his newly created rule did not apply in every case. Later I had the opportunity opportunity to read Claude Levi-Strauss' book, *The Savage Mind.* In it he presents some research findings concerning the thought processes of so called "savage" people. He makes the following points:

"Several thousand Coahuila Indians never exhausted the natural resources of a desert region in South California, in which today only a handful of white families manage to subsist. They lived in a land of plenty, for in this apparently completely barren territory, they were familiar with no less than sixty kinds of edible plants and twenty-eight others of narcotic, stimulant or medicinal properties.

. . . a single informant in the Gabon, recently developed an ethno-botanical list of about eight thousand terms, distributed between the languages or dialects of twelve or thirteen neighboring tribes.

. . . of a backward people of the Tyukyu archipelago, we read, 'Even a child can frequently identify the kind of tree from which a tiny wood fragment has come and furthermore, the sex of that tree, as defined by Kabiran notions of plant sex, by observing the appearance of its wood and bark, its smell, its hardness, and similar characteristics.' "

Because we tend to underestimate the capacities of others, it is necessary to have firsthand experiences in which we can come to discover what reality is. Naturally we can all read the same information. However, there is an affective component to the getting of information firsthand. Teachers in training need to experience people from other cultures as they exhibit cognitive complexity in order to have proper expectancies for teaching and learning and for a man-to-man respect for someone of another culture. Again, this will not happen automatically. Programs must be planned to insure that teachers do not overlook information.

Language

Communication is at the root of the problem of how to be a teacher. Recent advances in linguistic studies as applied to the field of education offer a great deal of promise for those who would be good teachers. The intercultural context is ideally suited for hypothesis testing in this area. Some form of basic linguistics is essential for teacher preparation and should not be left to chance. Our standard list of prerequisites needs to be reworked. Linguistics and education should be a part of basic teacher preparation and not simply reserved for the specialist. In that different cultures are best understood when we speak the language, not only linguistics but other languages should be required of teachers.

Learning and Culture

In the classic *Cultural Patterns and Technical Change,* Margaret Mead helped to focus attention on the way in which culture influences any normal human process.

Not only is resistance to change influenced by culture, but culture determines methods of conceptualization, as well as the raw data around which conceptualizations may be formed. Intercultural teacher preparation will permit teachers to focus on real situations in which culture makes a differential impact upon learners. Again, seeing and experiencing is believing. The exciting work of Michael Cole and John Gay on learning concepts among the Kpelle in Liberia, illustrates the degree to which culture and learning must be a topic for teachers.

Teacher Impact

In the intercultural context, the exaggerated behavior of the teacher can be noticed. The opportunity for peer feedback becomes more probable. Too often the subtle messages which teachers send to students are destined to remain at an unconscious level. However, the intercultural situation makes the teachers response pattern more visible.

Socioeconomic Status Impact

It is desirable that any intercultural setting for teacher preparation be structured so as to include more than one economic level of students. Specifically, the teacher should be made to examine the impact of socioeconomic status upon the interchange that takes place between the teacher and his students. For example, some studies have shown that many teachers have relatively little information about the poorest students in their classes. The key thing about this fact is that these teachers believe that they are responding to all children equally. Often teachers make other kinds of distinctions such as preferences for the academically talented. The intercultural setting can be used effectively to raise the level of teacher awareness in this area, since wide differences will tease out greater varieties of teaching behavior. Stanley Charnofsky in *Educating the Powerless* and Paulo Friere in *Pedagogy of the Oppressed* clearly document one aspect of the impact of social conditions on learning and teaching. These are things which teachers must see to believe.

The Teachers Own Feelings as an Influence

Ultimately the teacher has to be helped past the preliminary point of a clinical study of others. A teacher must be helped to become aware of his own subtle feelings, to find ways of dealing freely with children.

Program Development Principles

The implications of the foregoing for program development can be summarized as follows:

> *Planned use of cultural dissonance.* Cultural dissonance in the setting for the preparation program should be considered as an essential rather than as an enrichment activity. This is based upon the way in which the teacher can learn fully.

> *Foundations taught contextually.* It is necessary to think of psychology, sociology, anthropology, and philosophy of education as functional inquiries within a real context. The context itself should be the basic data for the disciplinary principles.

> *Teachers learn in groups.* Teams of trainees considering joint experiences and developing specific hypotheses for testing should be established. It is unlikely that a single teacher operating in isolation can encounter a sufficient variety of experiences or can interpret feedback without the benefit of peers. Trust is an indispensable element in the peer situation.

> *Multicultural staffing.* Multicultural staffing is not simply a matter of legal rights or moral principles. It is a fundamental pedagogical requirement. Relevant program planning and implementation can be achieved only with a culturally representative faculty. This does not mean that the same kind of multicultural representation is necessary for every program. Some diversity in training faculty is a positive institutional statement to all students.

Conclusion

We are responsible for teachers who are afraid of different students. We are responsible for teachers who have had no opportunity to come to know themselves in relationship to others. Most of all we are responsible if a teacher leaves us who goes into a classroom as a "tight little island" or an "encapsulated man". That teacher will never reap the reward of being a teacher and as a consequence, students will not meet a human being. The student may lose his opportunity to learn to live without fear and to crack his shell enough for the outside to pour in. Tight teachers and tight kids will mean that *WE BLEW IT!*

Chapter 17

FUND RAISING AND STAFF DEVELOPMENT: PROBLEMS AND SOLUTIONS REGARDING TWO MAJOR CONCERNS OF OVERSEAS SCHOOLS

John M. Bahner

This article is based on a working relationship with more than 100 American-sponsored overseas schools. During more than four years of association with the Office of Overseas Schools, U.S. Department of State, staff members of the Institute for Development of Educational Activities, the education affiliate of the Charles F. Kettering Foundation, have visited all but five of these schools and have conducted workshops overseas for staff members in over 40 of these schools.

Although this article deals with two major concerns common to all these schools, diversity within these schools is even more striking. Just as is true of schools in any state in the nation, American-sponsored schools overseas have a wide variety of pupil populations, wealth, educational practices, and ability to resolve their own problems.

During the past four years, it has become evident that there is a growing concern on the part of administrators and other staff members to make a conscientious effort to provide better education for American students overseas.

It would be easy for these schools to adopt a laissez-faire attitude regarding school improvement and claim that they not only have all the problems which confront stateside schools but also have additional adverse conditions (often overwhelmingly so) due to their distance from the United States and local governmental or financial restrictions. It is indeed commendable that many of them are engaging in concerted efforts to provide education more appropriate to the individual learners in their schools.

SUPPORTING INDEPENDENT, NONPROFIT, AMERICAN-SPONSORED OVERSEAS SCHOOLS

Financial Problems

In every major city throughout the world, there are hundreds of United States citizens between the ages of 5 and 19 who will remain in those cities for one to three years until their fathers are transferred back to the United States or to some other foreign country. They do not speak the language of the host country, and primarily for this reason their parents are concerned that these children will not get the schooling desired if they attend the host

161

country public schools. An obvious solution is for the American community to organize and support a school. In spite of the facts that the American population is constantly changing and there are no formal organizations or governmental units to provide either initiative or continuity, an informal American community endures. It establishes a school usually in the form of a non-profit organization with a board of directors comprised almost entirely of the parents.

There is no tax support for the school. There is no statutory assistance from business or industry. Corporations of U.S. origin or those of the host country have no legal obligation to provide financial support to the American-sponsored schools.

The schools are forced into a position of having tuition serve as their primary source of income. Unlike private universities or private pre-collegiate schools in the United States, endowment support is almost unheard of for these schools. Thus, tuition becomes a self imposed head tax — a condition most parents have never encountered previously except perhaps as an almost forgotten fact going back well over 100 years in American history. When these parents compare the tuition rate for a single child with the school tax on their last stateside real estate tax bill, they realize how much business and industry contributed to the support of their local schools. Families with more than one child wish they had heard of "population zero" when they were first married.

Obviously tuition rates have a practical ceiling because of the economic status of the parents. In some countries the government limits tuition rates for private schools, and in other countries the government imposes a legal limit at least for the host country nationals. American-sponsored schools which wish to include host country nationals in their student population either to maintain an economical size or because of their desire to have a cross cultural environment, find both the practical as well as the legal limits on tuition to be a serious handicap.

Moreover, there are additional financial costs in operating such schools because of various factors. For example, the bus transportation system to feed a single school must include the entire city and nearby suburbs. Remember, these schools are not in small towns but are in 100 of the largest cities in the world. Because of the language and nature of local books and materials, instructional supplies and equipment must be imported from the United States with resulting shipping costs and custom duties imposed. The severe time delay incurred in this process is not only aggravating, but can also be assessed as a financial factor if one considers the loss of productivity when such delays occur.

Another example of high unusual costs confronting American-sponsored overseas schools is the transportation costs incurred in moving a teacher from the United States. Although the payment of moving expenses is an extreme rarity for teachers moving from one system to another within the United States, it is almost mandatory if American-sponsored overseas schools are to attract the teachers they desire to fill their staff vacancies. Commonly, one way transportation is provided the first year, and if the teacher remains for a two-year contract, return transportation is paid at the end of that period. If the teacher signs another two-year contract, it is common practice to pay for a home leave for this teacher between the second and third years. Therefore, even if a teacher remains on a school staff and thereby provides a degree of continuity, these high transportation costs must be included in the school's budget.

Minimizing Financial Problems

As expenditures go up, provisions must be made to increase the income. The most direct means is to raise tuition. As indicated above, however, this has very real limitations both economically and legally. In most countries the U.S. dollar is diminishing in purchasing power and this usually means that tuition must be raised merely to maintain the status quo.

A common way for most American-sponsored overseas schools to minimize the professional payroll costs is to have a salary schedule with a double or triple standard. A U.S. trained teacher hired from the United States receives a salary roughly comparable to that in the United States. That is, the purchasing power of the salary in the local country is approximately equal to the purchasing power of an average teacher's salary in the United States. In most American-sponsored overseas schools, a second group of teachers is employed under the classification "local hire". Many of these are women educated in the United States and who are wives of business men or government officials living in the vicinity of the school and who have little or no work opportunities other than the school. Immigration and labor laws of the host country usually discourage and sometimes prohibit a foreigner from being hired in the school unless it can be shown that the talents needed of the prospective employee cannot be found in the host country labor market. In a few countries, this "local hire" classification has two divisions – one for U.S. trained teachers and one for non-U.S. trained teachers, with the latter receiving even lower salaries. In other countries the same effect is obtained with a two-standard salary schedule because host country nationals have less than the equivalent of a U.S. baccalaureate and therefore draw lower salaries due to this criterion. In any given school year, approximately ten percent of these 100 American-sponsored overseas schools engage in a fund raising activity. Most of these are for capital outlay purposes and are presented as a one-time appeal for funds to augment local building facilities. It is rare to find a school that has an annual fund raising drive for operating expenses.

These fund raising campaigns are directed toward parents (both past and current), alumini, and American corporations having interests in the area and which are most likely to need a school with a U.S. curriculum so that their own personnel willingly accept an assignment in that city.

In addition to tuition and special fund raising drives, a third source of income for American-sponsored overseas schools is in the form of special acts of Congress. These acts are analogous to the situation in the United States where a so called "impacted" area receives special federal funds on the presumption that the federal government has increased the school population without the school system being able to obtain proportionate revenue from its normal taxing efforts. In the case of American-sponsored overseas schools, the Congress has provided funds to help support schools where embassy, foreign aid, and other governmental employees are in attendance. The U.S. Department of State has set up an Office of Overseas Schools to assist these non-profit, non-sectarian, non-military American-sponsored overseas schools in receiving their share of these specially appropriated funds.

If one assumes that American school-aged children should receive the same federal support wherever they receive their schooling regardless of national boundaries, then several other means of governmental help appear on the horizon. Almost all of these U.S. children are in foreign countries because their parents are associated with the U.S. government, U.S. business, and U.S. industry — all of which supposedly are acting in the national interests of the United States. The fact that these children are forced to attend schools outside the United States should not prevent the schools they attend from being eligible for specialized legislation such as the Elementary and Secondary Education Act. Since there are no state or local governmental agencies to help support these American-sponsored overseas schools, it is reasonable to assume that the federal government has a responsibility to support the schooling of U.S. children with general financial assistance on an annual basis. Unfortunately, there is not even pending legislation to make such schools eligible for general assistance on a perpetual basis or eligible for specialized funding in the same manner as public schools within the United States.

Five years ago, the American business community joined forces with the U.S. Department of State's Office of Overseas Schools to create the Overseas Schools Advisory Council. One of the Council's first acts was to devise a plan known as "fair share" through which financial support — more than $1,000,000 over the past four years — is solicited from those businesses and foundations whose employees enroll their children in schools other than those operated by church organizations, private companies, and the U.S. Department of Defense.

Secondly, the Council selected /I/D/E/A/ to work with the professional staff of the schools to provide guidance in expenditure of these funds as well as to conduct programs of educational improvement. Through personal visits and consultation with the Department of State's regional educational officers and each overseas administrator, /I/D/E/A/ determines the most effective ways to use the "fair share" funds contributed to the Institute. Contributions are solicited by the Overseas Schools Advisory Council from each U.S. company and foundation whose employees have children attending these American-sponsored overseas schools. The amount of contribution requested is in proportion to the number of such children attending the schools involved. Contributions may be made in two ways, either directly to individual schools as desired by the company or to /I/D/E/A/. Money donated to /I/D/E/A/ is pledged to be used in direct benefit of the schools in its Overseas Schools Project.

STAFF DEVELOPMENT IN AMERICAN-SPONSORED OVERSEAS SCHOOLS

Inservice Education Problems

An average staff turnover rate of fifty percent is a major problem in providing a good inservice education program in American-sponsored overseas schools. At the same time this turnover rate also increases the need for inservice education as new staff members must become acquainted with the students and educational operation of the school as well as become attuned to the general culture in which they find themselves.

Although the percentage varies from well over fifty in many elementary schools to less than ten in high schools, the teaching staff of these American-sponsored overseas schools are not trained in colleges and universities of the United States. This diversity brings to the school both assets and liabilities, but increases the need for inservice education if only to provide staff members with knowledge of goals and methodologies used by their colleagues within the school.

Because of the difficulty in hiring staff members for many of these schools, a U.S. college graduate without professional training in education but who speaks the language is often preferred to a teacher who perhaps has professional training but does not have an adequate English language facility. Other staff members are hired who have had professional training in education but who have had little or no experience prior to being hired in the overseas school.

There is less tendency for teachers in overseas schools to attend "refresher" courses in U.S. universities during the summer time since they either prefer to travel abroad or to spend the time visiting with family and relatives if they return to the United States. Therefore, teachers who make a caaeer overseas tend to lack exposure to professional literature and current trends. Administrators especially tend to be career-oriented overseas and are less likely than their stateside counterparts to be able to provide the leadership needed in promoting innovations. (Fortunately, within the last several years there is an increasing trend for these administrators to obtain a year's leave of absence and return to the United States for additional training.)

Another adverse factor for staff members in American sponsored overseas schools is that they have little chance for professional interaction except with fellow teachers on their own staff. Magazines of professional associations are relatively expensive to ship overseas and they arrive months late. Conferences and other inservice activities through the school year are extremely rare except for meetings attended by the headmaster and perhaps a principal if the school is relatively rich.

Although a number of United States universities have overseas programs, they are usually undergraduate programs and not oriented to teacher education. If professional courses are available, they tend to be the traditional lecture type and therefore do little to improve the everyday operational procedures of the classroom. There are a few notable exceptions to this in recent years, but the generalization still applies.

Together with a high percentage of staff turnover, the nature of the children in American-sponsored overseas schools ranks in the category of major problems. Only the highly transient, inner-urban school in the United States has the corresponding degree of pupil transiency, language difficulties, wide range of learning aptitude, and extreme diversity of educational background. Just as is true for the inner-city schools in metropolitan United States, nothing is more inappropriate for the students of American-sponsored schools overseas than a traditional graded curriculum with predetermined expectations and subject matter sequence and a pace determined by textbooks or system-wide curriculum guides. Any realistic program of staff development must assist the teachers in making learning opportunities more appropriate to the individual student.

Surmounting Inservice Obstacles: Individually Guided Education Abroad

The partnership of /I/D/E/A/ and the Office of Overseas Schools together with its Overseas Schools Advisory Council was not merely a fund raising project. As mentioned earlier, funds are provided to individual schools to assist them in a school improvement program. A great emphasis has been placed by /I/D/E/A/ on staff inservice training opportunities to provide a stimulus toward innovative, yet valid, school improvement programs. Through its Overseas Schools Project, I/D/E/A/ is providing a comprehensive, two-year inservice training program for these schools. A single school would not be able to afford the knowledgeable persons and resource materials necessary to accomplish a task of this magnitude. However, with support from the Overseas Schools Project in the form of workshops, travel money, and teacher training materials, this cooperative venture continues to provide a unique inservice program for a number of schools.

Individually Guided Education (IGE) is a comprehensive set of innovative teaching and organizational concepts that strive to blend personalized planning for students and processes of continuous improvement into a total learning environment. The IGE inservice program provides printed documents, films, and filmstrips designed to help teachers create new organizational patterns and learning programs for individuals according to each student's capabilities, interests, and learning styles.

As a school staff first becomes involved with the IGE program, a primary emphasis is placed on a twelve-day clinical workshop which enables teachers and leadership personnel to learn specific planning, teaching, and self-improvement processes. The workshops are conducted in a school environment where participants work with students during the morning hours. Part of each afternoon is used by the participants to critique the morning's operations as a process for improvement. Input sessions and independent study pertaining to IGE as well as planning for the next day's teaching account for the balance of the day. Participants acquire skills needed for working in cooperative teaching endeavors and learn strategies for making the instructional program a highly personalized, individually-planned series of learning experiences. The program is designed to provide educators with a number of proven instructional processes and decision making procedures which all aid them in individualizing education for the pupils in their charge. The program is also designed to enable key staff members in the schools to assist their colleagues in implementing IGE.

The workshop is structured to provide common processes in the planning and management of learning thereby providing a sound basis for the continuity of the educational program regardless of the level or theater of operations. Teachers participate in working teams so that experience, talents, problems, and familiarity with overseas teaching can be shared. The IGE inservice program, which includes multi-media support materials, is intended to assist teachers in the art of training other teachers to implement the process. Since the participants return to their schools with the necessary IGE training materials, they are able to offer on-the-job training to new staff members without the need for outside consultants. Thus, IGE minimizes the adverse effects on overseas schools due to a high rate of pupil and teacher turnover and the resulting lack of continuity in the educational program.

Implementation of IGE began for the first time overseas in the summer of 1971 at workshops in Sao Paulo, Brazil and Singapore. The overseas IGE program calls for schools in a defined area to form a league so they can assist each other. Each league is organized around one school in an area which receives special inservice help from /I/D/E/A/ and gets a year's headstart on the other area schools in implementing IGE. This school then becomes a resource school to assist others in the region as they begin to implement IGE a year later. The league is designed to give the schools a means of continuous improvement. It does this by legitimatizing school change, providing status for members, and being a source of mutual support. Most importantly, it is a means of solving problems through the sharing of ideas and people to bring new insight and a fresh approach to the problems of any member school within the league.

During the 1971-72 school year, follow-up visits were made to Sao Paulo and Singapore and staffs from other schools in these two regions attended IGE workshops in the summer of 1972. In addition two new resource schools were initiated in Madrid, Spain and Bogota, Colombia. As during the previous year, follow-up visits were made in Madrid and Bogota to assist the respective staffs in implementing IGE and at the same time to identify additional schools in the respective regions to be involved in a workshop in the summer of 1973.

Since IGE materials have been produced only for schools serving ages 5-12, the workshops conducted thus far have been for elementary school personnel. Beginning in the summer of 1973, IGE for ages 10-15 will be available for junior high and middle schools. Identical procedures will be used in the same regions to assist schools to implement IGE for these age groups. It is anticipated that IGE implementation in high schools will commence in the summer of 1974.

Thus, more than 100 American-sponsored overseas schools are now capitalizing on the multi-million dollar effort of /I/D/E/A/ to investigate the processes in the change of schools and to develop programs of school improvement. /I/D/E/A/ does not intend to become a permanent consulting agency to the overseas schools. Rather, once /I/D/E/A/ has assisted the schools in initiating the IGE program, the Institute expects that these schools will become more self sufficient, will work cooperatively with other schools in their geographic region, and will establish significant relationships with universities and school systems in the United States which will help them continue their constant efforts to seek better ways of educating their students.

Chapter 18

EVALUATION OF AMERICAN OVERSEAS EDUCATIONAL PROGRAMS

David Churchman

Thousands of young Americans attend elementary and secondary schools and branches of higher educational institutions overseas. Thousands more spend summers or other short periods participating in various types of study abroad programs. Their individual educational experiences differ far more than they would in the United States,, since the added ingredients of other cultures, customs and characteristics provide a kaleidoscope of learning opportunities.

However, those unique and vital gems of understanding which are the added benefits of education overseas must be sifted and carefully weighed and measured to insure that the experience abroad does not lessen the opportunity for continued educational progress through the academic system in one's native country.

How can this sifting, weighing and measuring be accomplished in the best interests of the young scholar living away from his homeland? How can educational leaders obtain the appropriate information critical to their decision-making regarding this type of "transplanted" education, while still embuing their programs with embellishments of the cultural settings in which these programs exist?

When such questions are asked, a call may be placed to a researcher, a philosopher or an accrediting agency to rescue school leaders from their woes by telling them what they should continue, change, stop or add. However, none of these approaches will necessarily guarantee that a proper evaluation of the situation and its attendant problems will have been made prior to taking particular actions. Evaluation, simply stated, is the provision of information which is useful in making administrative decisions. It also necessitates the involvement of those about whom, for whom, and with whom the educational enterprise exists. Evaluations, unlike standard educational research activities, do not usually add to the general knowledge about the educational process. They are directed at sets of problems in extremely different educational situations in full consideration of the practicalities involved. Evaluations do not ordinarily incorporate many "normal" research techniques such as verification of results by frequent repetition of an experiment; elimination of alternative explanations for an observed phenomenon by careful control of extraneous variables; or selection, definition, and restriction of a problem which can be properly attacked by scientific methodology.

Educational evaluations usually deal with problems which have been raised by administrators who must rely on existing information, judgment, and the techniques of defining types of programs and types of decisions which must be made about them.

The four examples which follow will demonstrate the range and nature of evaluation of overseas American educational programs. Three of these studies were specifically developed from a model conceived by the Center for the Study of Evaluation at the University of California, Los Angeles. The Center was established by the United States Office of Education for the purpose of developing and improving evaluation theory and practice. The Center is now under the aegis of the National Institute of Education. Most evaluation models tend to be either theoretic models or practical models. The Center has been able to combine these two aspects of evaluation by using both theoretical researchers and applied researchers who constantly modify evaluation theories in the light of actual efforts to apply them in countless and highly diverse circumstances.

The first example involves the School-to-School Program. Established by the Office of Overseas Schools of the United States State Department in 1964, the School-to-School Program consisted of voluntary partnerships between a public school district in the United States and an American-sponsored overseas school.[1] Each partnership would explore ways by which the resources of the public schools could be brought to bear on the problems of the overseas schools, and ways in which the overseas school could help to intensify the international exposure of the public schools. In actuality, administrators from partnership schools met annually to exchange ideas and seek other ways in which the partnership idea could be developed. School board members and administrators visited their partner schools. Policies encouraging teacher exchanges were developed, exchanges of curriculum materials were planned, and student pen pal programs were begun. Other examples included one stateside district providing computer record-keeping for its partner, and one overseas school providing facilities and faculty to enable students from the stateside partner to experience a European study tour.

In spite of all the activity, the School-to-School Program did not live up to the original high hopes many had for it. Few readily-shared curriculum materials were actually developed and exchanged. Only one-tenth of one percent of the overseas school staffs were exchange teachers on leave from their stateside partner schools. Student, teacher and parental participation in

---

[1] Nonprofit, nonsectarian, coeducational schools located outside the United States and its territories, which meet a demonstrated need for providing facilities, curriculum and instruction for American children. The majority also enroll citizens of other countries.

the program was virtually nonexistent. Much of the activity was "ad hoc" rather than developmental aspects of a coherent long-range plan. Additionally many stateside partners felt that they were giving much more to the partnerships than they were getting in return. The surest indicator of the extent of the problems was the disolution of many of the partnerships each year.

The mixed record of successes and failures raised questions about the propriety of the goals originally established for the program. Administrators concluded that a more viable set of goals was needed. Nominally, the Program served students, parents, teachers and administrators of seventy American-sponsored overseas schools, and their counterparts in partnership school systems throughout the United States. A questionnaire which permitted the rating of the relative importance of a wide range of possible objectives by an "evaluator" for the School-to-School Program was developed. Two of the objectives are shown in Figure 1.

Figure 1

Facsimile Items from the Needs Assessment Instrument

SPECIAL ASSIGNMENT

The stateside school gives its teachers a chance to learn about the partnership school and country by assigning teachers each year to some of the jobs open in the overseas school. The teacher is paid by the overseas school, and also receives half of his regular pay. The year may be taken by the teacher in addition to his regular sabbatical leave.

Sabbatical leave; a leave, usually for one year, from his regular job during which a teacher improves his skills or learns new material to use in his regular job.

PEN PALS

To encourage students to exchange views, and to encourage international friendships, each student in the overseas school corresponds regularly (by mail, tape letters or other appropriate method) with a student in the stateside school.

Methods of political pollsters were used to select parents, U.S. students, teachers, administrators, and school board members to complete the questionnaire. By making the sample as representative as possible; by making the questionnaire comprehensive; by the evaluator visiting half the schools in Europe, the Near East and South Asia and their stateside partners; and by using an appropriate type of statistical analysis; 98% of the questionnaires were completed and a reasonably accurate estimate of opinion as to the most appropriate objectives for the Program was assembled. On the basis of the information collected, eleven basic goals were suggested for the Program. Five involved ways in which the stateside school could help its overseas partner. Three were ways in which the overseas school could help the stateside school. Three were general goals applicable to all partners. Each goal was a combination of two or more objectives which received high ratings from one or more groups of individuals in the sample. To aid in interpreting these recommendations, the evaluation report gave the relative importance attached to each objective and indicated specific groups of respondents, if any, which disagreed with that rating. Thus, administrators of the Program were given information which enabled them to judge the validity of the recommended goals, and to make decisions as to which ones to implement. This study[2] is one example of an evaluation conducted to provide administrators with information helpful to making decisions aimed at improving programs for which they are responsible.

A very different evaluation was performed to determine the value of an inservice seminar for teachers in India during the summer of 1970. One secondary school teacher from each of the fourteen districts in Bucks County, Pennsylvania, as well as a number of county school board members and administrators participated in the six-week seminar. The program included classroom presentations by Indian specialists on aspects of Indian society, as well as travel to historic, scenic, commmercial, industrial, and agricultural sites in northern India. The group also met numerous government officials, including Indira Gandhi who received the group at her home. One of each participant's assignments was an individual project which required an intensive investigation of some particular aspect of Indian life, such as cooking or business methods. To facilitate completion of the project, each participant actually lived in the home of an appropriate volunteer, such as an Indian housewife or bank executive for several days. The participants returned with over 4000 slides and an abundance of other material for

---

[2] Churchman, David, *A Needs Assessment Evaluation of the School-to-School Program in Europe, the Near East, South Asia and the United States,* unpublished dissertation, 1972.

classroom use, highly enthused by their experience. However anecdotes alone did not convince school board members that scarce financial resources should be used for the continuing support of the seminars abroad. Therefore, records were kept of such factors as the number of presentations teachers made to community groups, the number of courses and curricular units which teachers developed and implemented as a result of their experiences in India, the number of children who were introduced to Indian life through these materials, and so forth. The evidence that the seminar abroad was having a broad impact on the schools and the communities they served led to support of a similar seminar in 1971. This time, elementary school teachers participated in a program which stressed life in southern India. Similar evaluative data was again collected, and led to the conclusion that a third group of teachers should be selected for a 1972 seminar, but this time in Morocco. Thus, evaluation data provided the evidence needed to continue an innovative international program, which was of direct benefit to the entire citizenry of a large American community.

Another example of an evaluation is that designed for the Experiment in International Living. Among innovative educational programs for students, the Experiment in International Living provides high school and college age students the opportunity to live with a family in another country. The experiment is designed to help students learn behavior acceptable to that culture, and how to react to that culture in terms of its attitudes, beliefs, and values. The hope is that this experience will help the student to examine his own attitudes, beliefs and values with a broader and less rigid perspective, as well as to understand the ways in which his behavior as an American will be interpreted and misinterpreted in that culture.

The difficult questions were: "Are we reaching our objectives?" and "How can the program be improved?". Improvement of the program depended on determining the extent to which students achieved their objectives if they live with one type of family rather than with another. Collecting the data necessary to make such determinations involves complications which are characteristic of the problems of evaluation of programs in international education. For example, actual learning is confounded with the student's writing ability and "key" phrases remembered from the Experiment in International Living's brochures and pamphlets, thus making objective judgment difficult if essays are used for evaluation. In addition, the program serves such a large number of students that rapidly scoreable tests are required. Yet, objective tests are not amenable to measuring student reaction to the hundred of unexpected events which determine much of what the student learns overseas; they tend to be even more transparent as the "right" answers where attitudes are being measured. To complicate matters students vary greatly in their factual and intercultural knowledge, linguistic abilities, perceptions, and attitudes. Finally, the type of people with whom the student lives: a farmer, a professor, a factory foreman, etc.; the location: a capitol city, a large town, a rural community, etc.; and a host of other factors affect the opportunity which each student has to reach the objectives of the program. By determining which aspects of the program were most responsible for achieving objectives, and which aspects were making minimal or even negative contributions, the instruments developed provide a variety of sources of information which are useful in improving the extent to which the individualized educational program achieves the purpose for which it is intended.[3]

The general purpose of the three evaluations discussed above was to broaden or intensify intercultural knowledge and perspectives of Americans about other countries. This purpose is secondary to traditional academic preparation in schools serving Americans living abroad for extended periods of time. The fourth example of an evaluation was conducted for the schools operated by the Department of Defense (DOD) for dependents of American military personnel and civilian employees of the military stationed overseas. The formal testing program in these schools consisted of once-a-year administration of a battery of tests which generated a general IQ score and scores in mathematics, reading, science and social studies for all students in four grades. Teachers were expected to use individual test scores for individualizing instruction, and counselors were expected to use them for pupil personnel services. Summary data was computed for reports to Congress as to the quality of the education provided to overseas dependents. Complaints from all sides as to the inadequacy of this approach led to a moratorium of the testing program. An evaluation was conducted to identify the nature and extent of the complaints and the purposes, if any, for which individuals throughout the system needed test information.

Two methods were used to collect evaluation data. The first, a questionnaire, was designed to determine the relative importance of having information about various aspects of the curriculum. A 105-item question-naire was distributed and returned by 677 DOD secondary school personnel, and a 106-item questionnaire was sent to and completed by 846 elementary school teachers. The ratings led to the recommendations of fifteen elementary and nineteen secondary tests, and identification of additional areas in which testing should occur for which instruments were not currently available from publishers.

The second method was a structured interview administered to 338 teachers in twenty overseas schools as well as to thirty-five administrators at various levels of the DOD system.

---

[3] Churchman, David, *Report to Theodore Gochenour,* Experiment in International Living, October, 1971, unpublished.

Analysis of results led to recommendation of six purposes for which data from the thirty-six recommended tests should be used. Three of these pertained to decisions made by teachers, principals and counselors within schools; two pertained to information needed by District and Area administrators, curriculum and other specialists; and one provided for improved accountability to Congress for the accomplishments of the system. The evaluation report also included suggestions for the implementation and administration of a testing program to achieve each of the six purposes. [4]

As demonstrated by these four examples, evaluation can provide valuable information for a wide variety of problems faced by American education abroad. However, if an evaluation is to be useful in helping administrators to make educational decisions, the evaluator must know the types of information required by administrators, as well as a wide variety of techniques for collecting and analyzing such information. Evaluation models provide a systematic framework for the approach taken by individual evaluators.

With the exception of the Pennsylvania study, the evaluations cited follow the UCLA Center for the Study of Evaluation's, which defines evaluation as the process of determining the kinds of decisions which have to be made; selecting, collecting and analyzing information needed to make those decisions, and reporting this information to appropriate decision-makers.

The first evaluation, in which data was collected and analyzed in order to make a recommendation as to the most appropriate goals for the School-to-School Program, as well as the evaluation of the DOD testing program, are examples of the first important type of decision which administrators must make. The Center model calls this a *Needs Assessment Evaluation,* which involves stating potential educational goals or objectives, deciding which of these are of highest priority, and determining how well the existing educational program is meeting the high priority objectives. This information is used to identify needs which should be pursued in the future and could, if the evaluation method were selected, involve Program Planning Evaluation, which concerns selecting the most appropriate methods, material, facilities, personnel and equipment to reach agreed-upon goals with particular types of students.

The Experiment in International Living was interested in collecting information to modify its program to better achieve its goals. Such decisions require two types of evaluation — Implementation Evaluation and Progress Evaluation. The first, Implementation Evaluation, focuses on whether or not the procedures specified in the program plan are actually carried out in the

---

[4] David Churchman, Marvin Alkin, Ralph Hoepfner and Paul Bradley, *An Evaluation of the Testing Program of the Dependents Overseas Schools of the Department of Defense* (DAHC 15-73-C-0061), December, 1972. Unpublished.

intended manner. This involves investigating the degree to which the program plan is being conducted as expected in the field situation. On the other hand, Progress Evaluation is aimed at determining the extent to which the planned program is actually achieving the intended objectives. Implementation Evaluation acknowledges that planners cannot foresee all and that plans may have to be modified, perhaps in the direction of the "unofficial" changes of teachers in the field, if objectives are to be reached. The Bucks County evaluation was conducted to make an overall judgment as to the value of overseas educational seminars. It is an example of "Outcome Evaluation", which leads to final judgments regarding the general worth of a total program. All too often, "Outcome Evaluation" is the only type of evaluation performed, when it is too late to modify anything which transpired previously.

Words like evaluation, assessment, accountability, worth, analysis and the like are becoming popular educational terms. Yet, they are essential ones to use when addressing the education of American youth in foreign settings. Whatever evaluative techniques educational leaders of overseas programs select, first, they should encourage the concept of evaluation; second, they and their staffs, parents, and students should all be involved in the evaluation processes; and third, they should effect the type of educational climates which would encourage necessary change. What is right should be continued, but what is wrong must be corrected in the essential interest of young Americans away from their native country.

A FINAL NOTE

As the interaction and the interdependence of the nations of the world increases, the concerns of educators about cross-cultural and cross-disciplinary programs heighten. The gaps between ideologies and approaches must be bridged, with respect, and avoidance of infringing and imposing upon one anothers' views and methodology on how young people are best educated. We must share.

We have a vast, mass educational structure in the United States which has raised the level of our citizenry far beyond the expectations of its original designers. In many places, however, our schools are in chaos; they are patrolled by armed security officers; they have divided camps of management and labor, they are the campaign issues of politicians, and they are in financial and leadership trouble.

Yet, our schools are still the major hope for the future, both domestically and overseas. Our educators are the major crusaders who must expand the minds of young people to make such hope a reality. These young people are the reasons the ideas contained in this book have been assembled.

AMERICAN EDUCATION ABROAD

Autobiographical Sketches of Contributors

Part I

Donald K. Phillips

Executive Director of the Montreux, Switzerland-based European Council of International Schools, which publishes the ECIS Directory of International Schools and operates the ECIS Personnel Center for the placement of overseas teachers, Dr. Phillips was formerly a superintendent of schools in Vermont and New York. He has also served as Headmaster of the International School of Brussels, Belgium, and President of the American College of Switzerland.

Thomas T. Drysdale

Currently, Deputy Director, Directorate for Dependents Education, Department of Defense, Washington, D.C., and Director, Educational Planning and Development; Mr. Drysdale, who is overseas on a regular basis, spent 10 years in various positions abroad with the dependent schools.

Robert Leetsma

Associate Commissioner for International Education in the U.S. Office of Education, Dr. Leetsma has been the Director of the Institute of International Studies in U.S.O.E. since its establishment in 1968. He has a broad background of teaching, research, field experience, policy planning, and administration in international education.

William F. Sturner

Assistant President for Planning and Administration of Oakland University in Rochester, Michigan, Dr. Sturner also teaches in the Political Science Department. He is chairman of the Committee on Overseas Study Programs. Prior to his tenure at Oakland, he taught at the University of Detroit.

John E. Fobes

John Fobes is Deputy Director-General of UNESCO. He was previously Assistant Director-General and a visiting scholar at Indiana and Harvard Universities. He has served the United Nations and the U.S. Government, including the Marshall Plan and as Deputy Director of the U.S.A.I.D. Mission to India.

Paul Coste

Joining UNESCO in 1970, Mr. Coste has worked in teacher education, curriculum and structures of education. His special interests are in team teaching, non-graded schools, and curriculum reform. Additionally, he has served as a teacher and administrator in American schools abroad.

Raymond E. Schultz

Until recently the Director of the International Office of the American Association of Junior Colleges, Dr. Schultz is Professor of Community College Education at Washington State University. He has also taught at Florida State University and the University of Illinois. Author of one book and over 50 articles and special reports, he has numerous overseas experiences.

Robert J. Leach

Mr. Leach has devoted twenty-three years to the International School of Geneva, where he initiated the International Baccalaureate program. Among his publications is the Parcamon study of *International Schools*.

Part II

Thomas F. Kelly

Superintendent of the American Cooperative School in Monrovia, Liberia, until recently; Mr. Kelly was previously an Associate Director of the U.S. Peace Corps in Liberia. He is now engaged in doctoral study at Michigan State University emphasizing research relating to the educational implications of the mobile overseas American student.

Thomas E. Quinlan

Recently named Dean of Students at Loyola-Marymount University of Los Angeles, Dr. Quinlan was previously Chairman of the Department of Education at Marymount College. He spent three years as an Education Officer for the Ministry of Education in Kenya, and has taught in public schools in New York and California.

Blaise Donadio

Immigrating to the United States from Southern Italy, Dr. Donadio began formal teaching in the California Conservation Camps of Southern California and continued on in the adult education programs of the poorer sections of Los Angeles. Twenty-five years of teaching in secondary and junior college vocational programs followed. His continued studies in English as a Second Language led him to two years at the American University in Cairo.

Dennis L. Buckley

Dr. Buckley is a Lecturer in Education at the Riverina College of Advanced Education in Wagga Wagga, New South Wales, Australia. A comparative educationalist, he has taught languages in the United States in junior and senior high schools and both German and American students in Germany. He was a Fulbright scholar in Germany and conducted his doctoral research on the reform of the German secondary school.

Albert A. Chudler

Currently Principal of Canadian Academy in Kobe, Japan, Mr. Chudler has also served overseas as Superintendent of the International School of Kuala Lumpar in Malaysia. He is now on leave from the Los Angeles City Schools where he has served, respectively, as teacher, vice principal, and principal.

Thomas J. LaBelle

Dr. LaBelle is Assistant Dean for Research and Assistant Professor in the Graduate School of Education at UCLA. He has served in the Peace Corps, and written in the areas of anthropology and education, especially Latin American education, due to his continued work and research in that part of the world.

Val D. Rust

An Assistant Professor of Education in the area of comparative education at UCLA, Dr. Rust has an extensive background in teaching and research. He has worked with the Teacher Corps, teacher education programs and Head Start in Hawaii, and the Teacher Interchange Program.

Part III

Asa Hilliard

Dean of the School of Education at California State University, San Francisco, Dr. Hilliard was previously Chairman of the Department of Secondary Education. He was Acting Superintendent and Director of the University's Advisory Team to the Monrovia, Liberia Consolidated School System, after serving as a consultant to the Peace Corps and to the School System. He has taught on the junior and senior high school levels, and is a frequent speaker and consultant.

John M. Bahner

Dr. Bahner is Director, Division of Innovative Programs, /I/D/E/A/, which is sponsored by the Kettering Foundation, and is currently emphasizing the development of inservice programs for teachers. He has been an Associate Superintendent of Schools, an Assistant Professor of the Harvard Graduate School of Education, and a public school teacher and administrator.

David Churchman

A member of the senior research staff of UCLA's Center for the Study of Evaluation, Dr. Churchman has taught school in Morocco, Pennsylvania, and California. He has conducted educational evaluations for the Department of Defense Dependents Overseas Schools, the American Association of School Administrators, the Office of Overseas Schools of the U.S. State Department and the states of Hawaii and New Mexico.

William G. Thomas

Dr. Thomas is currently Dean of UCLA's Experimental Education Programs. As Dean of Educational Career Services and Director of UCLA's Administrative Fellowship Program, Dr. Thomas coordinated the University's educational placement activity, both in the U.S. and abroad, as well as related programs and projects. Formerly Dean of Students at San Fernando Valley State College, Dr. Thomas has also headed the UCLA placement program in business and industry and has taught at several Southern California colleges and universities.

His interests in international education evolved primarily from two years spent in Germany as a civilian working in cultural and recreational affairs for the U.S. Forces in Europe. Recently, he made an extended trek throughout Europe gathering information relating to educational employment opportunities for Americans. He is an author, frequent speaker and consultant in student affairs and personnel management areas. He resides with his wife and four sons in Northridge, California.